ONE POT

ONE POT

hamlyn

Published in the UK in 1998
by Hamlyn, a division of Octopus Publishing Group Ltd
2–4 Heron Quays, London E14 4JP

This edition published 2002 by Octopus Publishing Group Ltd

ISBN 0 600 60826 3

Printed in China

NOTES

Both metric and imperial measurements have been given in all
recipes. Use one set of measurements only and not a
mixture of both.

Standard level spoon measurements are used in all recipes.
1 tablespoon = one 15 ml spoon
1 teaspoon = one 5 ml spoon

Eggs should be medium unless otherwise stated.
The Department of Health advises that eggs should not be
consumed raw. This book contains dishes made with raw or
lightly cooked eggs. It is prudent for more vulnerable people
such as pregnant and nursing mothers, invalids, the elderly,
babies and young children to avoid uncooked or lightly cooked
dishes made with eggs. Once prepared, these dishes should
be kept refrigerated and used promptly.

Meat and poultry should be cooked thoroughly. To test if poultry
is cooked, pierce the flesh through the thickest part with a
skewer or fork – the juices should run clear, never pink or red.

Milk should be full fat unless otherwise stated.

Do not re-freeze a dish that has been frozen previously.

Pepper should be freshly ground black pepper unless
otherwise stated.

Fresh herbs should be used unless otherwise stated. If
unavailable, use dried herbs as an alternative but halve the
quantities stated.

Measurements for canned food have been given as a standard
metric equivalent.

Nuts and nut derivatives
This book includes dishes made with nuts and nut derivatives.
It is advisable for customers with known allergic reactions to
nuts and nut derivatives and those who may be potentially
vulnerable to these allergies, such as pregnant and nursing
mothers, invalids, the elderly, babies and children, to avoid
dishes made with nuts and nut oils. It is also prudent to check
the labels of pre-prepared ingredients for the possible inclusion
of nut derivatives.

Contents

Introduction

This varied collection of recipes draws on the expertise of many nations in creating delicious, tasty dishes that can all be cooked on the hob, mainly in one large pot. There is a tempting range of recipes to choose from. You will find hearty, substantial soups and stews from all over the world, creamy risottos and pasta dishes, couscous recipes from North Africa, tempting steamed dishes from the Far East and traditional steamed puddings as well as some unusual Thai desserts.

An ideal and versatile utensil for stove-top cooking is a multi-pot set of stainless steel pans (below). This comprises a large pan for cooking stews and casseroles, stocks and soups, and an additional section which fits over it and is used for steaming. The big pan comes with a perforated liner which fits snugly inside and enables a large quantity of pasta to be cooked and drained simply by lifting it out. The well-fitting lid ensures that no heat escapes during cooking.

Alternatively, you could use heavy-based saucepans, with well-fitting lids, so that food needing long, slow cooking can be left unattended without the risk of burning. If it is not possible to obtain a very low setting on your hob, a heat diffuser can be set under the pan, so that the dish can be left to cook slowly and safely.

A large steamer greatly increases the range of dishes that you can cook on the hob, as it can be used for such widely different foods as oriental dumplings, North African couscous and English sponge puddings. And of course steaming vegetables will conserve their flavour and nutrients.

Don't worry if you do not have a special couscous pot or couscoussier, it is possible to cook couscous just as successfully in a conventional steamer. However, do remember that you will need to put a piece of folded muslin in the steamer tray to prevent the fine couscous grains from falling through the perforations.

Once you get the knack of one-pot cooking you'll find that it's easy and fun to stack different layers of utensils and cook different dishes over one basic pot. In fact, stove-top cooking is

ideal for modern life styles. Standard cookers with large ovens were popular in the days when large families ate together every day and many house-wives did their own baking. These days many cooks find that cooking on the hob is more convenient and less costly than heating up the oven to cook one dish.

SPECIALIST INGREDIENTS

The ingredients used in these recipes have been chosen to give the best possible flavour. Occasionally, some more unusual ingredients such as kaffir lime leaves, galangal, Thai sweet basil and saffron threads are used in order to achieve the most authentic flavours. These ingredients are available from large supermarkets and specialist oriental food stores.

PREPARING FOOD

SKINNING TOMATOES

Cut a shallow cross at the stem end of each tomato. Put them in a bowl and pour over enough boiling water to cover. Leave for 1–2 minutes, then drain and peel off the skin.

HANDLING CHILLIES

Fresh chillies need careful preparation. The hottest parts are the seeds, and most recipes require you to remove every single one. Cut the chillies in half lengthways and scrape them out with a small, sharp-pointed knife.

Be careful to keep your hands away from your eyes, as the tiniest drop of chilli juice will cause an acute burning sensation. Wash your hands well after-wards, as well as the knife and board. If the skin of your hands is sensitive to the chilli juice, wear rubber gloves, or rub oil into them before starting.

CLEANING SQUID

The edible parts of squid are the body sac and tentacles. The head and innards are discarded.

1 Hold the squid in one hand and pull the head and tentacles sharply away from the body with the other. This will bring most of the innards with it. Pull out the transparent backbone and scrape out any remaining innards.

2 Peel the thin purplish skin off the body sac and discard. Rinse the body cavity well, drain and pat dry. Cut into rings or chunks.

3 Cut the tentacles off the head, wash, pat dry and cut into pieces.

MAKING SPRING ONION TASSELS

Spring onion tassels can make an attractive garnish. They are very easy to make but need to be prepared in advance.

1 Cut off a 7.5 cm/3 inch piece of green stalk. Finely slice the top leaves down their length, leaving 2.5 cm/1 inch uncut at the base.

2 Immerse in iced water until the sliced leaves open out and curl over to form the tassel.

PREPARING CRAB MEAT

1 Break the legs of the crab and crack the shells into 2 or 3 pieces.

2 Open the shell by laying the crab on its back and pressing down with your thumbs along the suture. Lift out and discard the stomach, intestine and feathery gills. Crack the shell with a chopper or heavy knife.

3 Clean the shell, legs and claws of all crab meat, taking care to separate the white meat from the dark meat.

SAUCES AND DRESSINGS

The exotic flavours of oriental and Middle-eastern dishes are often used in special sauces and dressings. These can be found in large supermarkets or specialist food stores, but it's easy and fun to make your own.

HARISSA PASTE

1 Deseed 50 g/2 oz of fresh red chillies. Put them in a bowl, cover with boiling water and leave to soak for 30 minutes.

2 Drain and put them in a spice grinder or mortar with 3 crushed

garlic cloves, 1½ teaspoons of coriander seeds and 1 teaspoon each of salt, caraway seeds, mint and cumin. Add 1–2 tablespoons of olive oil and work to a paste.

3 Spoon the mixture into a clean dry jar and drizzle with a little extra oil to seal. Store in the refrigerator.

SWEET AND SOUR DRESSING

1 Put 1 shredded spring onion in a large screw-top jar with 2 finely diced plums. Add 5 tablespoons olive oil, 2 tablespoons sherry vinegar, 2 teaspoons soy sauce, 2 teaspoons tomato purée, ½ crushed garlic clove and ¼ teaspoon soft light brown sugar. Season to taste with salt and pepper, then shake well to combine the ingredients.

GARLIC MIXTURE

1 Crush enough garlic cloves to fill 2 tablespoons. Put them in a mortar

with 2 tablespoons of chopped coriander root or stem and a heaped teaspoon of pepper. Pound all the ingredients together until they are well blended and have formed a paste. The flavour is enhanced if the mixture is prepared 1–2 days in advance and stored in the refrigerator.

COCONUT CREAM AND MILK

1 Put 400 g/13 oz grated fresh or desiccated coconut into a saucepan with 900 ml/1½ pints of milk. Bring to the boil, then lower the heat and simmer, stirring occasionally, until the mixture has reduced by one-third.

2 Strain through a sieve, pressing the mixture with a wooden spoon to extract as much liquid as possible. Pour the strained milk into a bowl, allow to cool, then refrigerate. When it is cold skim off the thicker 'cream' that rises to the surface. The remaining liquid is the coconut milk.

HOMEMADE STOCKS

While stock cubes have their place, the flavour of a fresh, homemade stock is far preferable. They are easy and cheap to make, using only a few basic ingredients. Once cooked and cooled the stocks can be frozen ready for use when needed. Freeze in small batches in ice cube trays and then transfer the cubes to labelled plastic bags for ease of storage. Use beef, chicken and vegetable stock within 3 months; fish stock within 2 months.

To make good stock remember to simmer it as gently as possible, or it will evaporate too quickly and become cloudy. Never add salt to stock as the long simmering process will reduce and concentrate the flavour. This will affect the flavour of the final dish. Remove any scum that rises to the surface, otherwise it will spoil the colour and flavour of the stock.

BEEF STOCK

Preparation time: 15 minutes
Cooking time: about 4½ hours

This is a simplified version of classic beef stock, made without bones so that it cooks more quickly.

1 Cut 750 g/1½ lb boned shin of beef into cubes and place them in a large saucepan. Roughly chop 2 onions, 2–3 carrots and 2 celery sticks and add to the pan with 1 bouquet garni (2 sprigs of parsley, 2 sprigs of thyme and 2 bay leaves) and 4–6 black peppercorns. Pour in 1.8 litres/3 pints of cold water.

2 Bring slowly to the boil, then reduce the heat to a slow simmer. Cover with a well-fitting lid and simmer for 4 hours, skimming off any scum when necessary.
3 Strain the stock through a muslin-lined sieve and leave to cool before refrigerating.

Makes about 1.5 litres/2½ pints

CHICKEN STOCK

Preparation time: 5–10 minutes
Cooking time: about 2½ hours

1 Chop a raw or cooked chicken carcass into 3–4 pieces and place in a large saucepan with any other trimmings. Roughly chop 1 onion, 2 large carrots and 1 celery stalk and add them to the pan with 1 bay leaf, a few lightly crushed parsley stalks, and 1 thyme sprig. Cover with 1.8 litres/3 pints of cold water.
2 Bring the stock to the boil and skim off any scum that rises to the surface. Lower the heat and simmer for 2–2½ hours.
3 Strain the stock through a muslin-lined sieve and leave to cool before refrigerating.

Makes 1 litre/1¾ pints

FISH STOCK

Preparation time: 10 minutes
Cooking time: 20 minutes

When buying the bones for this stock avoid those from oily fish. It is also very important that the stock does not boil.

1 Place 1½ kg/3 lb fish trimmings in a large saucepan along with 1 sliced onion, the white part of 1 small leek, 1 celery stalk, 1 bay leaf, 6 parsley stalks, 10 whole peppercorns and 475 ml/16 fl oz dry white wine. Cover with 1.8 litres/3 pints of cold water.
2 Bring slowly to just below boiling point. Simmer gently for 20 minutes, removing any scum from the surface.
3 Strain the stock through a muslin-lined sieve and leave to cool before refrigerating.

Makes 1.8 litres/3 pints

VEGETABLE STOCK

Preparation time: 5–10 minutes
Cooking time: about 45 minutes

The vegetables used in this stock can be varied according to your taste and what you have available. Do not use potatoes or any other floury root vegetables as they will tend to make the stock cloudy.

1 Place 500g/1 lb of chopped mixed vegetables (for example, equal amounts of celery, leeks, onion and carrots) in a large saucepan with 6 peppercorns, 1 garlic clove and 1 bouquet garni. Cover them with 1.2 litres/2 pints of cold water.
2 Bring to the boil, then simmer gently for 30 minutes, skimming off any scum when necessary.
3 Strain and set aside to cool before refrigerating.

Makes 1 litre/1¾ pints

Hearty Soups

Making soup at home is extremely satisfying and surprisingly quick and easy. Substantial soups like these, packed with fresh vegetables, flavoured with bacon, cheese or seafood and enriched with rice, pulses or potato, are complete meals in themselves. The only equipment you need is a heavy-based pan with a well-fitting lid, so that the soup can be simmered gently with minimum evaporation of liquid.

Onion and Cheese Soup

The addition of the Parmesan and Gruyère cheeses makes this a substantial soup – serve it with crusty bread and a green salad for a simple meal.

Preparation time: 20 minutes
Cooking time: 35–40 minutes

- 2–3 tablespoons olive oil, plus extra for frying
- 1 kg/2 lb onions, thinly sliced
- 50 g/2 oz plain flour
- 1.2 litres/2 pints Chicken Stock (see page 9)
- 2 slices stale bread, crusts removed, cut into 1 cm/½ inch cubes
- 50 g/2 oz Parmesan cheese, grated
- 50 g/2 oz Gruyère cheese, cut into small dice
- salt and white pepper

TO GARNISH:
- cracked black peppercorns
- flat leaf parsley sprigs

1 Heat 2–3 tablespoons of oil in a large heavy-based pan and add the onions. Cook gently until they are soft but not coloured. Stir in the flour, mix well and then add the stock a little at a time, stirring until smooth. Season to taste with salt and white pepper. Bring to the boil and simmer gently for *20 minutes*.

2 Meanwhile, prepare the croûtons. Heat some oil in a frying pan. When hot, add the bread and fry until golden brown, turning the cubes frequently with a spatula so they colour evenly. Remove from the pan with a slotted spoon and drain on kitchen paper.

3 Purée the soup in a food processor or blender (in batches if necessary), and return to the pan. Alternatively, rub the soup through a sieve. Just before serving add the Parmesan and Gruyère. Heat through and cook for *2–3 minutes*, stirring constantly. Check the seasoning and serve immediately in individual bowls. Garnish each one with a few croûtons, some cracked black peppercorns and parsley.

Serves 4–6

Hearty Bean Soup

Preparation time: 20 minutes
Cooking time: 30 minutes

- 1 celery stick, chopped
- 1 large carrot, chopped
- 1 large onion, chopped
- 2 x 425 g/14 oz cans red kidney beans
- 1 tablespoon olive oil
- 400 g/13 oz can chopped tomatoes
- 2 tablespoons chopped flat leaf parsley
- 2 garlic cloves, chopped
- ½–1 teaspoon chopped rosemary
- 600–900 ml/1–1½ pints hot Chicken Stock (see page 9) or water
- 75 g/3 oz arborio rice
- salt and pepper
- 25–40 g/1–1½ oz Parmesan cheese, grated, to serve
- rosemary sprigs, to garnish

1 Put the celery, carrot and onion in a heavy-based pan, just cover with water and simmer for *15 minutes*. Add the drained beans, reserving 4–6 tablespoons. Pour the vegetables and liquid into a bowl and set aside.

2 Heat the oil in the pan and add the tomatoes, parsley and garlic and cook gently until the mixture thickens. Add the rosemary and salt and pepper to taste. Add the beans and vegetables and their liquid and cook for 5 minutes or until tender. Purée in a food processor or blender, in batches if necessary, or rub through a sieve.

3 Make up the purée to 1.5 litres/2½ pints with stock or water. Season to taste. Return to the pan and add the rice. Bring to the boil and simmer for *15–20 minutes* until the rice is cooked. Add the reserved beans and a little water if necessary – this should be a very thick soup. Heat through then garnish with the Parmesan and rosemary.

Serves 4–6

Mussel Soup

Preparation time: 30 minutes
Cooking time: 30 minutes

- 2.5 litres/4 pints mussels
- 1 bouquet garni
- 450 ml/¾ pint water
- 125 ml/4 fl oz red wine
- 3 tablespoons olive oil
- 1 large onion, chopped
- 2 garlic cloves, crushed

- 2 x 400 g/13 oz cans chopped
  tomatoes
- pinch of sugar
- few saffron threads
- salt and pepper
- small bunch of flat leaf
  parsley, chopped, to garnish

1 Prepare the mussels: cover them with cold water and discard any that are open or float to the surface. Scrub the remaining mussels under cold running water and remove the beards.

2 Place the mussels in a large heavy-based pan with the bouquet garni, 150 ml/¼ pint of the water and the red wine. Cover with a tightly fitting lid, bring to the boil and then cook over a medium heat for a few minutes until the mussels open, shaking the pan occasionally. Strain the mussels, reserving the cooking liquid, and set aside. Discard any mussels that have not opened.

3 Heat the oil in the cleaned pan and fry the onion and garlic until soft but not coloured. Add the tomatoes, sugar and salt and pepper to taste, then stir well. Add the reserved mussel liquid and the remaining water, and crumble in the saffron. Bring to the boil and then simmer for *15 minutes*.

4 Remove most of the mussels from their shells and add to the pan, together with the mussels in their shells. Heat through gently and adjust the seasoning if necessary. Serve in warm soup plates, garnished with parsley.

Serves 4

Thai Tomato and Prawn Broth

Classic Thai ingredients are much easier to find now, making authentic dishes a real possibility. Large supermarkets and oriental stores should provide those listed below.

Preparation time: 20 minutes
Cooking time: 1 hour

- 500 g/1 lb raw tiger prawns
- 1 red chilli, bruised
- 3 lemon grass stalks, roughly chopped, or grated rind of 2 lemons
- 4 kaffir lime leaves, or 1 tablespoon grated lime rind
- 4 slices of fresh root ginger
- 2 sprigs of coriander
- 900 ml/1½ pints Vegetable Stock (see page 9)

- 2 tablespoons sunflower oil
- 1 small onion, chopped
- 2 garlic cloves, sliced
- 1 teaspoon grated fresh root ginger
- 2 x 400 g/13 oz cans chopped tomatoes
- 2 tablespoons dark soy sauce
- 12 large basil leaves

1 Peel the prawns, reserve the meat and place the heads and shells in a large heavy-based pan. Add the chilli, lemon grass or lemon rind, lime leaves or rind, sliced root ginger, coriander and stock. Bring to the boil, cover and simmer gently for *30 minutes*.

2 Heat the oil in a large heavy-based pan and fry the onion, garlic and grated ginger for *5 minutes*. Add the tomatoes and simmer gently for a further *5 minutes*. Strain the prawn shell stock and add it to the tomatoes along with the soy sauce; bring to the boil, cover and simmer gently for *10 minutes*. Add the prawns and simmer gently for a further *5–6 minutes* or until cooked. Serve the soup in bowls topped with the basil.

Serves 4

Chickpea Soup

Preparation time: 15 minutes
Cooking time: 2½ hours

- 1 small smoked boneless bacon hock joint, about 500–750 g/1–1½ lb
- 1 onion studded with 4 cloves
- 2 garlic cloves, crushed
- 1 bay leaf
- 1 sprig of thyme
- 1 sprig of marjoram
- 1 sprig of flat leaf parsley
- 1.8 litres/3 pints Chicken Stock (see page 9)
- 300–375 g/10–12 oz potatoes, cut into 1 cm/½ inch cubes
- 300 g/10 oz Savoy cabbage, shredded
- 150 g/5 oz canned chickpeas, drained
- pepper

1 Put the bacon joint in a very large, heavy-based pan and cover with cold water. Bring the water briefly to the boil, then drain, discarding the water.

2 Return the bacon joint to the cleaned pan. Add the onion, garlic, bay leaf, thyme, marjoram, parsley and stock. Bring the mixture to the boil, then lower the heat and simmer, partially covered, for *1½ hours*. Remove and discard the onion, bay leaf and sprigs of thyme, marjoram and parsley. Lift out the bacon, place it on a board and cut it into small pieces. Set the pieces aside.

3 Add the potatoes and cabbage to the pan and simmer for *30 minutes*. Add the chickpeas and reserved bacon pieces to the soup and cook for *10 minutes* more. Season with pepper to taste and serve in warm soup bowls.

Serves 8–10

Variation
Marrowfat Pea and Ham Soup

Preparation time: 10 minutes, plus soaking
Cooking time: 2–3 hours

1 Soak 250 g/8 oz dried marrowfat peas in cold water overnight.

2 Put a small smoked bacon joint into a large heavy-based pan and cover with cold water. Bring the water briefly to the boil, then drain.

3 Return the bacon joint to the cleaned pan and pour in 1.5 litres/2½ pints water. Drain the peas and add to the pan with 1 chopped onion, 1 crushed garlic clove, 2 chopped celery sticks and 1 bouquet garni. Cover and boil rapidly for *10 minutes*, then simmer gently for *2–3 hours*, until the peas are soft. Remove the bouquet garni.

4 Cool slightly, then remove the bacon joint and chop into bite-sized pieces. Return the pieces to the pan, season to taste with pepper and reheat gently.

White Onion Soup

Preparation time: 15 minutes
Cooking time: about 1 hour

- 50 g/2 oz butter
- 500 g/1 lb onions, very thinly sliced
- 1 leek, white part only (about 50 g/2 oz), thinly sliced
- 40 g/1½ oz plain flour
- 1 litre/1¾ pints Chicken Stock (see page 9)
- 150 ml/¼ pint single cream, plus extra to garnish
- salt and white pepper
- croûtons, to serve

1 Melt the butter in a large heavy-based pan. Add the onions and leek. Cover tightly and cook over a low heat, stirring frequently, for about *30 minutes*. Do not allow the onions and leek to brown.

2 Sprinkle the flour over the onions and leek and stir well to mix. Gradually add the stock. Bring to the boil, then reduce the heat and simmer for *15 minutes*.

3 Season the soup with salt and pepper to taste, add the cream and reheat without boiling. Serve garnished with a swirl of cream and croûtons on top.

Serves 4–6

Variation
Red Onion Soup

Preparation time: 10 minutes
Cooking time: 1 hour

1 Heat 3 tablespoons oil in a large heavy-based pan, add 3 large sliced red onions, 1 sliced fennel bulb and a crushed garlic clove. Cook gently for *5 minutes*. When the vegetables begin to soften, sprinkle with a little salt, cover and cook for *30–35 minutes*. Increase the heat, add 2 tablespoons red wine vinegar and boil for *1–2 minutes* until the liquid is reduced by half.

2 Add 1 bay leaf, 2 sprigs of thyme, ½ teaspoon crushed peppercorns, 150 ml/¼ pint red wine and 600 ml/1 pint Chicken Stock (see page 9). Bring to the boil, reduce the heat and simmer for *10–15 minutes*. Remove the thyme and bay leaf and adjust the seasoning to taste. Serve topped with crumbled goats' cheese and croûtons.

Serves 4

Callaloo Soup

Preparation time: 15 minutes
Cooking time: 35–40 minutes

- 3 tablespoons oil
- 1 large onion, finely chopped
- 4 spring onions, chopped
- 2 garlic cloves, crushed
- 1 red chilli, deseeded and finely chopped
- 1 teaspoon turmeric
- 1 thyme sprig, finely chopped
- 250 g/8 oz okra, trimmed and thinly sliced
- 500 g/1 lb fresh callaloo or spinach leaves, trimmed and coarsely chopped
- 900 ml/1½ pints Chicken Stock (see page 9)
- few saffron threads
- 400 ml/14 fl oz canned coconut milk
- 250 g/8 oz crab meat, fresh or canned
- juice of ½ lime
- dash of hot pepper sauce
- salt and pepper

1 Heat the oil in a large, heavy-based pan and add the onion, spring onions and garlic. Fry gently for *5 minutes*, or until softened. Add the chilli, turmeric and thyme, and stir over a low heat for *1–2 minutes*.

2 Stir in the okra and then add the chopped callaloo or spinach leaves. Turn up the heat and cook, stirring, until the leaves start to wilt. Reduce the heat and add the chicken stock and saffron. Bring to the boil, then cover and simmer for *20 minutes*.

3 Add the coconut milk and crab meat and stir well. Heat gently for *4–5 minutes*, then season to taste with salt and pepper. Just before serving, stir in the lime juice and hot pepper sauce.

Serves 6

Jamaican Pepperpot Soup

Preparation time: 30–35 minutes
Cooking time: 1½ hours

- 1 kg/2 lb lean stewing beef, cut into small cubes
- 250 g/8 oz lean pork, cut into small cubes
- 2.5 litres/4 pints water
- 24 okra, trimmed and chopped
- 500 g/1 lb kale, chopped
- 2 green peppers, deseeded and chopped
- 500 g/1 lb spinach, chopped
- 2 spring onions, chopped
- 500 g/1 lb yellow yams, thinly sliced
- 1 large potato, thinly sliced
- 1 garlic clove, finely chopped
- 1 thyme sprig
- ½ teaspoon cayenne pepper
- salt

1 Combine the beef and pork with the measured water in a large heavy-based pan. Bring to the boil, then lower the heat and simmer, partially covered, for about *30 minutes*.

2 Add the okra, kale, peppers, spinach and spring onions to the pan with the thyme and cayenne. Cook over a medium heat, partially covered, for *15 minutes*. Add the yams, potato and garlic and cook for a further *20 minutes*, or until the yams and potato are soft. Add more water if the soup is too thick. Season with salt to taste and serve in warm soup bowls.

Serves 6–8

Smoked Haddock Chowder

The chowder, now widely regarded as an American dish, stems from the French word '*chaudière*' which relates to the cauldron or kettle in which French peasants had been cooking long before the discovery of America.

Preparation time: 10–15 minutes
Cooking time: 35 minutes

- 500 g/1 lb potatoes, cut into 1 cm/½ inch cubes
- 1 onion, finely chopped
- 1 bay leaf
- ½ teaspoon chopped marjoram
- 600 ml/1 pint water
- 500 g/1 lb skinned smoked haddock fillet, chopped
- ¼ teaspoon ground nutmeg
- 450 ml/¾ pint milk
- white pepper

TO GARNISH:

- 2 tablespoons finely chopped marjoram
- croûtons (optional)

1 Combine the potatoes, onion, bay leaf and marjoram with the measured water in a large heavy-based pan. Bring the mixture to the boil, then lower the heat, cover and simmer for *5 minutes*.

2 Add the chopped haddock, nutmeg and milk to the pan, with white pepper to taste. Simmer the soup, partially covered, for *20 minutes*.

3 Serve the chowder in warm soup bowls, garnished with marjoram and croûtons, if using.

Serves 4–6

Potato and Bacon Soup

Preparation time: 20 minutes
Cooking time: 1 hour

- 175 g/6 oz smoked bacon rashers with rinds on
- 1 tablespoon olive oil
- 1 onion, finely chopped
- 2 garlic cloves, finely chopped
- 600 ml/1 pint Chicken Stock (see page 9)
- 1.2 litres/2 pints water
- 750 g/1½ lb potatoes, diced
- 3 leeks, sliced
- 1 teaspoon chopped marjoram
- ½ teaspoon ground nutmeg
- 1 teaspoon Worcestershire sauce
- 3–4 tablespoons finely chopped flat leaf parsley (optional)
- salt and pepper

1 Cut the rinds off the bacon and set them aside. Roughly chop the bacon rashers.

2 Heat the oil in a large heavy-based pan and cook the bacon rinds over a medium heat until crisp, then remove them with a slotted spoon and discard.

3 Add the chopped bacon, onion and garlic to the fat remaining in the pan and cook over a medium heat for *8–10 minutes* or until the onion is light brown and the bacon fairly crisp. Stir frequently.

4 Add the stock, measured water, potatoes, leeks, marjoram, nutmeg and Worcestershire sauce to the pan, with pepper to taste. Bring the mixture to the boil, lower the heat, cover and simmer for *25 minutes*, stirring from time to time.

5 Put 600 ml/1 pint of the soup mixture in a food processor or blender and blend for about *2 seconds*, until roughly blended. Alternatively, mash with a potato masher. Return the mixture to the pan, stir well and cook the soup for *10 minutes* over a low heat. Add salt to taste. Just before serving stir in the parsley, if using. Serve in warm soup bowls or plates.

Serves 8

Spicy Apple and Potato Soup

Preparation time: 10–15 minutes
Cooking time: about 25 minutes

- 50 g/2 oz butter or margarine
- 1 small onion, diced
- 2 dessert apples, peeled, cored and sliced
- pinch cayenne pepper or more, to taste
- 600 ml/1 pint Vegetable Stock (see page 9)
- 300 g/10 oz potatoes, thinly sliced
- 300 ml/½ pint hot milk
- salt

TO GARNISH:
- apple slices, fried in butter (optional)
- cayenne pepper

1 Melt the butter or margarine in a large heavy-based pan and cook the onion for *5 minutes*, or until softened. Stir frequently. Add the apples and cayenne and cook for a further *2 minutes*, stirring constantly. Pour in the stock, then add the potatoes. Bring to the boil, lower the heat and simmer for *15–18 minutes* or until the apples and potatoes are very soft.

2 Purée the soup in a food processor or blender until it is very smooth – you will have to do this in batches. Return the puréed soup to the pan.

3 Reheat the purée and stir in the hot milk. Cook very gently over a low heat for a few minutes to heat through. Taste and adjust the seasoning. Serve the soup in warm bowls, garnished with the fried apple slices, if using, and a light sprinkling of cayenne.

Serves 4–6

Variation
Curried Apple and Potato Soup

Replace the cayenne pepper with 1 tablespoon curry powder – mild, medium or hot according to your taste. Fry the curry powder with the onion in step 1, to develop its flavour. Then continue with the main recipe.

Steamed Dishes

Steaming is a very healthy way to cook, as no fat is used, and vegetables keep all their vitamins and flavour. Thai cooks know the value of this method, and use it for meat-filled dumplings, seafood parcels and aromatic curries. A steamer can be a simple collapsible platform which fits a range of saucepans, or a rigid type with its own lid. The new stainless steel multi-pots have well-fitting steaming compartments. For Thai recipes you might try the multi-layered bamboo steamers.

Prawn Parcels

Preparation time: 30 minutes
Cooking time: 8–10 minutes

- 2 garlic cloves
- 1 shallot, chopped
- 5 cm/2 inches fresh galangal root, peeled and chopped
- 1 lemon grass stalk, finely chopped
- 3 kaffir lime leaves, chopped
- 1 teaspoon dried red chilli flakes
- 2 teaspoons chilli oil
- 1 tablespoon *nam pla* (Thai fish sauce)
- 1 tablespoon lime juice
- ¼ teaspoon caster sugar
- 75 ml/3 fl oz coconut milk
- 24 raw prawns, peeled and deveined, tails left intact

TO GARNISH:
- spring onions, sliced into strips
- ½ red pepper, cored, deseeded and sliced into strips

1 Place the garlic, shallot, galangal, lemon grass, kaffir lime leaves, chilli flakes, chilli oil, *nam pla*, lime juice and sugar in a food processor or blender and grind to a thick paste. Alternatively, pound with a pestle in a mortar. Add the coconut milk to the spice paste and mix well.

2 Place the prawns in a bowl and add the coconut spice mixture. Stir to coat the prawns evenly. Butter 4 large pieces of greaseproof paper. Place 6 prawns and a quarter of the coconut mixture in the centre of each piece. Wrap up to enclose the prawns, forming neat parcels.

3 Steam the prawn parcels over a pan of boiling water for *8–10 minutes*.

4 To serve, remove the prawns from the parcels and place on 4 serving plates. Pour the coconut mixture into a bowl and whisk briefly until smooth. Pour a little over each portion, garnish with spring onions and red pepper strips and serve immediately.

Serves 4

Steamed Crab in the Shell

Preparation time: 10 minutes, plus cooling
Cooking time: 25 minutes

- 4 crab shells, washed and dried
- 2 tablespoons chopped fresh coriander
- 2 red chillies, deseeded and thinly sliced
- 2 eggs, beaten
- oil, for deep-frying
- coriander sprigs, to garnish
- chilli sauce or *nam pla* (Thai fish sauce), to serve

FILLING:
- 75 g/3 oz crab meat
- 75 g/3 oz raw prawns, minced
- 250 g/8 oz minced pork
- 1 egg
- 1 tablespoon Garlic Mixture (see page 8)
- 1 tablespoon *nam pla* (Thai fish sauce)
- 1 tablespoon soy sauce

1 First prepare the filling: mix the crab meat, prawns and pork together in a small bowl. Stir in the egg, garlic mixture, *nam pla* and soy sauce, and mix together well.

2 Pack the filling mixture into the crab shells and place them in a steamer over a large saucepan of boiling water. Scatter with coriander and strips of red chilli. Steam for *15 minutes*, then set aside to cool.

3 Carefully dip the cooled crab shells, filled side down, into the beaten egg.

4 Heat the oil in the large pan and deep-fry the crab shells, one at a time, for *1–2 minutes* or until the egg coating is golden. Remove with a slotted spoon and drain on kitchen paper. Garnish with coriander sprigs and serve with chilli sauce or *nam pla*.

Serves 4

Thai Steamed Fish Curry

Steaming is a delicious way of cooking fish curry. This gentle cooking process ensures that the fish is delicately cooked while remaining moist.

Preparation time: 10 minutes
Cooking time: 15 minutes

- 3 tablespoons Thai red curry paste
- 200 ml/7 fl oz coconut milk
- 1 tablespoon *nam pla* (Thai fish sauce)
- 1 egg, beaten
- 500 g/1 lb skinless cod or halibut fillets, cut into 5 cm/2 inch pieces
- 1 tablespoon chopped coriander
- 1 tablespoon chopped mint
- 1 tablespoon chopped Thai sweet basil
- 4 kaffir lime leaves, finely sliced
- 1 large green chilli, deseeded and finely sliced
- 1 large red chilli, deseeded and finely sliced
- plain boiled rice, to serve

1 Mix together the Thai red curry paste, coconut milk, nam pla and beaten egg. Set aside.

2 Place the fish pieces in a shallow non-metallic dish. Add the coriander, mint and Thai sweet basil and gently mix together to combine thoroughly. Pour the curry paste mixture over the fish and stir to coat evenly.

3 Scatter the kaffir lime leaves and chilli slices over the fish. Cover the dish with foil and steam over boiling water for *15 minutes* or until the fish is just cooked through. The sauce should be lightly thickened due to the addition of the egg. Serve immediately with the rice.

Serves 4

Variation

Steamed Fish Curry with Red Shrimp Paste

Preparation time: 10 minutes

1 Instead of using bought Thai red curry paste make your own hot paste. Deseed and slice 6 fresh red chillies. Place in a mortar with 2 teaspoons salt and pound to a paste. Add 1 tablespoon finely chopped spring onion and 2 teaspoons shrimp paste and pound until smooth.

2 Continue as in the main recipe, using the red shrimp paste in place of the Thai red curry paste.

Stuffed Squid

Preparation time: 20 minutes
Cooking time: 15 minutes

- **200 g/7 oz minced pork**
- **½ teaspoon Garlic Mixture (see page 8)**
- **1 tablespoon** *nam pla* **(Thai fish sauce)**
- **16 baby squid, cleaned, heads reserved**
- **1 egg, beaten**
- **25 g/1 oz dry breadcrumbs**
- **oil, for deep-frying**

TO GARNISH:
- **lemon slices**
- **coriander sprigs**

TO SERVE:
- **chilli sauce**
- **½ mooli, shaved into ribbons (optional)**

1 Place the pork in a bowl with the garlic mixture and *nam pla* and mix well. Fill each squid with some of this mixture and replace the heads, securing them in place with wooden cocktail sticks. With a skewer or sharp cocktail stick, pierce the skin around the tail of each squid in 2 or 3 places to let out air while they cook.

2 Arrange the stuffed squid in the top of a steamer over a large pan of boiling water. Place over boiling water and steam for *10 minutes*. Allow the squid to cool, then remove the cocktail sticks.

3 Put the beaten egg in one shallow dish and the breadcrumbs in another. Heat the oil in a large pan. Dip each stuffed squid first in the egg and then in the breadcrumbs. Deep-fry until crisp, remove with a slotted spoon then drain on kitchen paper. Garnish with lemon slices and coriander sprigs. Serve immediately with chilli sauce and a salad of raw mooli, if liked.

Serves 4

Dumplings with Pork and Prawns

Preparation time: 20 minutes, plus resting
Cooking time: 10–12 minutes

- 5½ tablespoons sunflower oil

DOUGH:

- 500 g/1 lb plain flour
- 175 ml/6 fl oz boiling water
- 125 ml/4 fl oz cold water

FILLING:

- 500 g/1 lb minced pork
- 500 g/1 lb raw prawns, peeled and minced
- 125 g/4 oz spring onion, finely chopped
- 1 tablespoon shredded fresh root ginger
- 1 tablespoon light soy sauce
- 1 bunch watercress, chopped
- ½ teaspoon salt
- pepper

DIPPING SAUCE:

- 2 tablespoons wine vinegar
- 2 tablespoons soy sauce

Serves 4–6

1 To make the dough, place the flour in a bowl with the boiling water, beat well until smooth, then leave to rest for *2–3 minutes*. Add the cold water and knead well.

2 Mix the filling ingredients together along with 1 tablespoon of the oil. Roll the dough into a long sausage shape and cut it into 4 cm/1½ inch lengths. Roll each one flat to make small pancake shapes. Place 1 tablespoon of filling on each pancake then fold it in half. Pinch the edges together to seal.

3 Heat 3 tablespoons of oil in a large heavy-based pan. Arrange the dumplings evenly in the pan. Turn the heat to high and shallow-fry the dumplings for *2–3 minutes*.

4 Add the cold water to the pan, cover and steam the dumplings over a high heat until almost all the water has evaporated. Remove the lid and pour in 1½ tablespoons of hot oil, drizzling it from the side. Reduce the heat and cook until all the liquid has evaporated.

5 Mix the vinegar and soy sauce to make a dipping sauce.

Variation

Dumplings with Pork and Ginger

Preparation time: 20 minutes, plus resting
Cooking time: 20 minutes

1 Follow step 1 of the recipe.

2 To make the dumpling filling, combine 500 g/1 lb minced pork with 1 tablespoon Chinese wine or dry sherry, 3 tablespoons soy sauce, 2 teaspoons sugar, 1 tablespoon sesame oil and 1 teaspoon each salt, cornflour and shredded fresh root ginger.

3 Roll out the dough and make and fill the pancakes as in step 3 of the main recipe.

4 Lay the dumplings 1 cm/½ inch apart on a piece of damp muslin in a steamer. Cover and steam vigorously for *20 minutes*. Serve with the dipping sauce.

Steamed Mussels in White Wine Sauce

Preparation time: 20 minutes
Cooking time: 10 minutes

- 2 kg/4 lb mussels
- 50 g/2 oz butter
- 1 large onion, finely chopped
- 1–2 garlic cloves, finely chopped
- 1 small leek, white and green parts, finely sliced
- 300 ml/½ pint dry white wine
- 150 ml/¼ pint water
- 25 g/1 oz plain flour
- 2 tablespoons finely chopped flat leaf parsley
- 1–2 tablespoons double cream (optional)
- salt and pepper

1 Prepare the mussels, cover them with cold water and discard any that are open or float to the surface. Scrub the remaining mussels under running water and remove the beards with a sharp knife.

2 Melt half the butter in a very large heavy-based pan and gently fry the onion, garlic and leek until soft but not coloured. Add the mussels, wine and measured water, cover and bring to the boil. Cook for *2–5 minutes* until the mussels open, shaking the pan several times during the cooking. Divide the mussels between 4 large soup bowls, discarding any that have not opened during cooking. Keep hot.

3 Mix the remaining butter with the flour to form a paste and little by little add to the juices in the pan, stirring to thicken.

4 Bring the mussel liquid to the boil, season with salt and pepper to taste, stir in the parsley and pour over the mussels. For extra richness, 1–2 tablespoons double cream can be added to the sauce just before serving, if you like.

Serves 4

Curry in Artichoke Cups

In Thailand this dish would be served in containers made from banana leaves; artichoke cups look equally attractive and are much easier to obtain.

Preparation time: 20 minutes
Cooking time: about 45 minutes

- 8 small globe artichokes

FILLING:

- 1½ tablespoons *nam pla* (Thai fish sauce)
- 150 g/5 oz minced pork
- 3 tablespoons coconut cream
- ½ teaspoon cornflour
- 250 ml/8 fl oz canned coconut milk
- 1½ tablespoons Thai red curry paste
- 1 egg, beaten
- 25 g/1 oz shredded cabbage, blanched
- 15 g/½ oz Thai sweet basil
- ½ tablespoon shredded kaffir lime leaves
- ½ red chilli, deseeded and thinly sliced

1 To prepare the artichoke cups, remove the outer leaves and trim the base of each globe artichoke so that it will stand upright. Wash in cold water, then cook in boiling water for *3–5 minutes*. Drain, then cut away and discard the chokes to create edible containers.

2 To make the curry filling, first place the *nam pla* in a shallow dish, add the minced pork and set aside.

3 Gently heat the coconut cream in the pan. Meanwhile, place the cornflour in a cup and mix to a paste with 1 teaspoon of the coconut milk. Stir this paste into the coconut cream and bring to the boil, stirring constantly. When it thickens remove it from the heat and set aside.

4 In a large bowl, mix half of the reserved coconut milk with the Thai red curry paste. Add the marinated meat, stirring constantly with a wooden spoon so that the meat and milk mixture are thoroughly mixed. Stir in the egg and gradually add the rest of the coconut milk.

5 Mix together the cabbage and Thai sweet basil leaves and divide the mixture between the artichokes. Carefully pour the curry mixture into the artichoke cups and top each artichoke with about 1½ teaspoons of the thickened coconut cream.

6 Carefully place the filled artichokes in the top of 1 or 2 steamers, packing them closely together, and sprinkle with shredded kaffir lime leaves and chilli slices.

7 Steam the artichokes over boiling water for *30 minutes*. Then, using a slotted spoon, carefully transfer them to a serving platter. Serve immediately.

Rainbow of Seasonal Vegetables

This recipe makes the perfect accompaniment to any kind of meat; or serve it on its own sprinkled with grated cheese, grilled until golden brown and accompanied by fresh crusty bread.

Preparation time: 20 minutes
Cooking time: 5 minutes

- 50 g/2 oz butter
- 1 tablespoon chopped herbs, such as mint and parsley
- 4 courgettes, cut in half lengthways
- 2 leeks, trimmed, washed and sliced
- 2 large carrots, cut into thick matchsticks
- 125 g/4 oz French beans, topped and tailed
- 4 celery sticks, cut into thick matchsticks
- small bunch of watercress, trimmed
- salt and pepper

1 Mix the butter with the herbs and season well with salt and pepper. Place the courgettes, leeks, carrots, beans and celery in a steamer, then season well with salt and pepper.

2 Cover and steam over boiling water for *3–5 minutes*. Add the watercress and steam for *1 minute* further. Turn on to a warm serving dish and dot with the herb butter.

Serves 4

Variation
Seasonal Vegetable Parcels

Preparation time: 20 minutes
Cooking time: 10 minutes

1 Prepare the vegetables as in the main recipe.

2 Fold 8 sheets of greaseproof paper in half. Cut a semi-circle of 15 cm/6 inch radius through each piece so that when opened out you have eight 30 cm/12 inch rounds of paper. Place the circles together in pairs so that you have 4 double-thickness circles.

3 Divide the vegetables between the 4 circles, arranging them on top of the 2 layers. Top one with a knob of butter and a strip of lemon rind, then sprinkle with white wine and some chopped herbs. Season well with salt and pepper. Fold the free half over to make a parcel. Fold the edges of the layers of paper over twice together, twisting and pressing hard to make an air-tight seal. Lay the parcels in a steamer. Cover with a tightly-fitting lid and steam over boiling water for *8–10 minutes*.

Stews and Casseroles

Simmering meat or poultry in stock with vegetables and herbs gives unsurpassed flavour and tenderness. Cooking times may be long, but little attention is needed, and if potatoes or dumplings are added you have a complete one-pot meal. Casseroles and stews can both be cooked on the hob. For long cooking, it is best to use a heavy-based pan with a well-fitting lid. You can use the main pot of the multi-pot sets very successfully.

Navarin of Spring Vegetables

Preparation time: 20–25 minutes
Cooking time: 25 minutes

- 250 g/8 oz small broad beans
- 175 g/6 oz mangetout, trimmed
- 175 g/6 oz fine young asparagus, trimmed and cut into 2.5 cm/1 inch pieces
- 75 g/3 oz butter
- 8 spring onions, thinly sliced
- 2 garlic cloves, chopped
- 900 ml/1½ pints Chicken or Vegetable Stock (see page 9)
- 1 thyme sprig
- 15 baby onions, peeled
- 10 baby turnips or 3 small turnips, cut into wedges
- 250 g/8 oz baby carrots, scrubbed
- 1½ tablespoons lemon juice
- salt and pepper
- chervil sprigs, to garnish

1 Blanch the broad beans, the mangetout and the asparagus separately in salted boiling water for *1 minute*. Refresh immediately in cold water. Drain and set aside.

2 Melt the butter in a large heavy-based pan over a low heat, add the spring onions and garlic and cook, without colouring, until softened. Add the stock and thyme, bring to the boil, then add the baby onions. Cover and simmer for *5 minutes*.

3 Add the turnips, bring back to the boil, then reduce the heat and simmer for *6–8 minutes*. Add the carrots and cook for *5–6 minutes*. Season with salt and pepper and stir in the lemon juice. Add the blanched vegetables and heat through. Serve garnished with chervil sprigs.

Serves 4

Variation
Navarin of Winter Vegetables

Preparation time: 30 minutes
Cooking time: 45 minutes

1 Melt 40 g/1½ oz butter in a flameproof casserole and fry 6 small onions for *3 minutes*. Add 500 g/1 lb diced potatoes, 225 g/8 oz thinly sliced carrots, and 250 g/8 oz diced celeriac, cover and cook over a low heat for *10 minutes*. Stir in 125 g/4 oz sweetcorn kernels, 900 ml/1½ pints vegetable stock and 2 bay leaves. Cover and simmer for *20 minutes*. Discard the bay leaves and season with salt and pepper.

2 Purée half the stock and vegetables in a food processor or blender. Stir into the original pan and add 125 g/4 oz diced Wensleydale or feta cheese and 2 tablespoons chopped parsley. Reheat gently and serve hot, scattered with croûtons and grated Parmesan cheese.

Silverside with Dumplings

Preparation time: 30 minutes
Cooking time: 2–2½ hours

- oil, for frying
- 1.75–2 kg/3½–4 lb silverside of beef, tied into a neat shape
- 1 onion, stuck with 6 cloves
- 1 bouquet garni
- 600 ml/1 pint water
- 300 ml/½ pint stout
- 12–16 small pickling onions
- 500 g/1 lb small carrots

DUMPLINGS:
- 125 g/4 oz self-raising flour
- 50 g/2 oz shredded suet
- 2 tablespoons finely chopped flat leaf parsley
- 1 large egg, beaten with 4 tablespoons cold water
- salt and pepper

1 Heat a little oil in a large heavy-based pan and brown the meat. Add the onion, bouquet garni, water and the stout. Bring to the boil, then simmer for *2 hours* or until the meat is tender. Three-quarters of the way through the cooking time, remove the onion and herbs and add the vegetables.

2 Meanwhile, make the dumplings. Sift the flour into a bowl, stir in the suet and parsley and season with salt and pepper, then mix to a dough with the egg and water. About *15 minutes* before the end of the cooking time, roll the dough into small balls and drop them into the simmering liquid.

3 Serve the meat on a warm serving plate surrounded by the vegetables and dumplings. Serve with boiled Brussels sprouts, if liked and serve some of the cooking liquid in a sauceboat.

Serves 6

Vegetable Stew with Herb Dumplings

Preparation time: 10–20 minutes
Cooking time: 40 minutes–1 hour

- 2 tablespoons oil
- 1 large onion, sliced
- 2 large carrots
- 3–4 celery sticks
- 175 g/6 oz turnips
- 500 g/1 lb potatoes
- 400 g/13 oz can tomatoes
- 750 ml/1¼ pints Vegetable Stock (see page 9)
- 1 tablespoon tomato purée
- 1 teaspoon paprika

- 4 tablespoons finely chopped flat leaf parsley
- salt and pepper

DUMPLINGS:

- 50 g/2 oz butter
- 125 g/4 oz self-raising flour
- 2 tablespoons finely chopped flat leaf parsley
- ½ teaspoon dried thyme or marjoram
- 1 egg, lightly beaten

1 Heat the oil in a large heavy-based pan and gently fry the onion until soft. Cut the carrots, celery, turnip and potatoes into 2.5 cm/1 inch cubes and add to the onion. Cover tightly and cook over a low heat for *5 minutes*. Add the tomatoes, stock, tomato purée, paprika and half of the parsley. Season with salt and pepper, bring to the boil, then simmer gently for *15–20 minutes*.

2 Meanwhile, prepare the dumplings. Rub the butter into the flour until it resembles fine breadcrumbs. Add the herbs, and season with salt and pepper. Mix with the egg and enough water to form a sticky dough. When the stew has been simmering for *15–20 minutes*, using a wet spoon, drop tablespoons of the dough on to the simmering stew. Cover and cook for a further *20–30 minutes*, until the vegetables are tender. Serve hot, garnished with the remaining parsley.

Serves 4

Variation
Chinese Vegetable Casserole

Preparation time: 15 minutes, plus soaking
Cooking time: 30–40 minutes

1 Soak 25 g/1 oz Chinese mushrooms in boiling water for *15 minutes*. Drain, discard the stalks and chop the caps finely. Heat 2 tablespoons oil in a heavy-based flameproof casserole, add 1 finely chopped onion and cook gently until soft.

2 Mix together 2 teaspoons cornflour, 1 tablespoon light soy sauce, 300 ml/½ pint vegetable stock and ½ teaspoon five-spice powder. Pour into the casserole. Add the mushrooms with 250 g/8 oz whole baby sweetcorn, 125 g/ 4 oz beansprouts and a 250 g/8 oz can bamboo shoots, drained. Bring to the boil, then taste and adjust the seasoning. Cover and cook over a very low heat for *10 minutes* or until the vegetables are just tender.

3 Add 125 g/4 oz mangetout and simmer for a further *10 minutes*, until they are cooked but still crisp.

Chicken in Red Wine

Preparation time: 15–20 minutes
Cooking time: 1½ hours

- 2 tablespoons oil
- 50 g/2 oz butter
- 2.5 kg/5 lb chicken, cut into 12 portions
- 24 small pickling onions, peeled
- 125 g/4 oz smoked bacon, diced
- 1 tablespoon plain flour
- 1 bottle Burgundy or other good red wine
- 1 bouquet garni
- 2 garlic cloves, unpeeled
- pinch of sugar
- freshly grated nutmeg
- 24 button mushrooms
- 1 tablespoon brandy
- salt and pepper
- 2 tablespoons finely chopped thyme, to garnish
- fried bread triangles, to serve (optional)

1 Heat the oil and butter in a large heavy-based pan and add the chicken pieces. Fry over a low heat until golden on all sides, turning occasionally. Remove the chicken from the pan with a slotted spoon and keep warm. Pour off a little of the fat from the pan, then add the pickling onions and bacon. Fry until lightly coloured, then sprinkle in the flour and stir well.

2 Pour in the wine and bring to the boil, stirring. Add the bouquet garni, unpeeled garlic cloves, sugar, nutmeg, and salt and pepper to taste. Return the chicken to the casserole, lower the heat, cover and simmer for *15 minutes*.

3 Add the mushrooms and continue cooking gently for a further *45 minutes* or until the chicken pieces are cooked and tender. Remove with a slotted spoon and arrange on a warm serving plate. Keep hot. Pour the brandy into the sauce and boil, uncovered, for *5 minutes* until thick and reduced. Remove and discard the bouquet garni and garlic cloves.

4 Pour the sauce over the chicken and garnish with chopped parsley. Serve with fried bread triangles, if liked.

Serves 6–8

Provençal Fish Stew

Preparation time: 30 minutes
Cooking time: 25–30 minutes

- 1 kg/2 lb firm white fish, such as cod or haddock, trimmed and cut into large pieces
- 500 g/1 lb firm potatoes, peeled and thickly sliced
- 600 ml/1 pint Fish Stock (see page 9)
- 2 egg yolks
- 300 ml/½ pint garlic mayonnaise
- 6–8 slices French bread, toasted or fried
- 2 tablespoons finely chopped flat leaf parsley, to garnish

1 Put the pieces of fish and the potatoes in a large heavy-based pan and pour in the stock. Cover the pan and bring to the boil. Reduce the heat and simmer gently for *15 minutes* or until the fish and potatoes are cooked. Remove them with a slotted spoon and transfer to a large warm dish.

2 Beat the egg yolks into half of the garlic mayonnaise. Add a little of the stock and mix well together.

3 Return to the pan with the rest of the stock and cook gently over a low heat, stirring constantly, until the sauce is thick enough to coat the back of a spoon. Pour the sauce over the fish and potatoes.

4 To serve, place 1–2 slices of French bread in each warm soup bowl. Spoon some fish and potatoes in their sauce on top. Garnish with chopped parsley and serve the remaining garlic mayonnaise separately.

Serves 4–6

Variation
Oriental Fish Stew

Preparation time: 20 minutes
Cooking time: 15–20 minutes

1 Cut 500 g/1 lb firm white fish fillets into small pieces. Mix 1 tablespoon cornflour to a paste with 2 tablespoons water. Stir into an egg white and use to coat the fish. Chop 500 g/1lb firm bean curd or tofu into small cubes.

2 Line a flameproof casserole with a few Chinese leaves or Cos lettuce leaves. Add the fish, bean curd, 3 tablespoons sake or dry sherry, 2 tablespoons light soy sauce, 1 teaspoon sugar, 2 slices peeled fresh root ginger and 3 chopped spring onions. Season with salt and pepper to taste.

3 Pour over 300 ml/½ pint fish stock and sprinkle in 50 g/2 oz chopped ham. Bring to the boil, then reduce the heat and simmer for *15–20 minutes*. Season lightly with sesame oil.

Catalan Pork Stew

Preparation time: 20 minutes
Cooking time: 1¼ hours

- 150 ml/¼ pint olive oil
- 750 g/1½ lb lean pork, cut into 2.5 cm/1 inch cubes
- 1 large onion, peeled and sliced
- 2 garlic cloves, crushed
- 400 g/13 oz can chopped tomatoes
- 1 green pepper, cored, deseeded and chopped
- 1½ teaspoons paprika
- 150 ml/¼ pint Chicken Stock (see page 9)
- salt and pepper
- 1 tablespoon chopped fresh coriander, to garnish

1 Heat 2 tablespoons of the olive oil in a large heavy-based pan, add the pork and fry gently until golden brown on all sides, turning occasionally. Remove from the pan with a slotted spoon.

2 Add the onion and garlic to the cooking juices in the pan and cook until soft and golden. Return the meat to the pan, and stir in the tomatoes, green pepper, paprika and stock. Season with salt and pepper. Bring to the boil, cover tightly and simmer gently for *1 hour* or until the meat is tender.

3 Serve the pork garnished with coriander. Plain boiled rice can be served with it if you wish.

Serves 4

Goulash

Goulash originated in Hungary and later became a very popular dish in Austria. Although there are many variations, paprika and caraway seeds are essential, giving the dish its unique aroma and flavour.

Preparation time: 15 minutes
Cooking time: 1¼ hours

- 3 tablespoons oil
- 750 g/1½ lb boneless lean beef, cut into 2.5 cm/1 inch strips
- 2 onions, chopped
- 2 garlic cloves, crushed
- 2 celery sticks, thinly sliced
- 3 tablespoons paprika
- 1 tablespoon caraway seeds
- 900 ml/1 pint Beef Stock (see page 9)
- ¼ teaspoon dried thyme
- 2 bay leaves
- ¼ teaspoon Tabasco sauce, or to taste
- 3 tablespoons tomato purée
- 250 g/8 oz potatoes, diced
- 3 carrots, diced
- 4–6 teaspoons soured cream (optional)

1 Heat the oil in a heavy-based pan and brown the meat in batches over a medium heat. As each batch browns, transfer it to kitchen paper to drain. Cook the onions, garlic and celery in the remaining oil until transparent.

2 Take the pan off the heat and stir in the paprika, caraway seeds and stock. Add the thyme, bay leaves, Tabasco and tomato purée. Stir well and add the beef. Bring the mixture to the boil, then lower the heat and simmer, partially covered, for *30 minutes*.

3 Add the diced potatoes and carrots and simmer for a further *30 minutes*, or until the potatoes are tender. Serve immediately in warm bowls, garnishing each portion with a teaspoon of soured cream, if liked.

Serves 4–6

Variation
Vegetable Goulash

Preparation time: 20 minutes
Cooking time: 1¼–1¾ hours

1 Heat 2 tablespoons oil in a flameproof casserole, add 1 large chopped onion and cook gently until soft. Add 1 tablespoon paprika, 1 teaspoon caraway seeds and cook for *1 minute*. Add a 400 g/13 oz can of chopped tomatoes and bring to the boil.

2 Add 1 large green pepper, deseeded and chopped, then 225 g/8 oz each sliced carrots, diced potatoes, and diced pumpkin or squash. Season to taste, cover the casserole and bring to the boil. Simmer very gently for *1–1½ hours*, stirring occasionally. If necessary, add a little water or stock.

3 Stir in 150 ml/5 fl oz soured cream and reheat gently without boiling.

Lamb Shanks with Olives and Sun-dried Tomatoes

The saffron mash makes a splendid accompaniment to the lamb shanks, emphasizing its Mediterranean origins. However, the lamb may also be served with crusty bread, if you prefer.

Preparation time: 25 minutes
Cooking time: 2–2½ hours

- 4 lamb shanks, about 500 g/1 lb each
- 2 tablespoons plain flour
- 2 tablespoons olive oil
- 2 red onions, sliced
- 2 tablespoons rosemary leaves
- 3 garlic cloves, chopped
- 100 ml/3½ fl oz balsamic vinegar
- 200 ml/7 fl oz red wine
- 50 g/2 oz pitted black olives, quartered
- 40 g/1½ oz sun-dried tomatoes, cut into strips lengthways
- 175 ml/6 fl oz water
- salt and pepper

SAFFRON MASH:

- 1 kg/2 lb potatoes, cut into large chunks
- 100 ml/3½ fl oz single cream
- large pinch of saffron threads
- 5 tablespoons extra virgin olive oil

1 Toss the lamb in the flour, shaking off any excess. Heat the oil in a heavy-based pan large enough to hold the lamb shanks in one layer, over a medium heat. Add the lamb and brown well all over. Remove and set aside.

2 Reduce the heat, add the onions and cook for about *10 minutes* until softened. Add the rosemary and garlic and cook for a further *2–3 minutes*. Increase the heat, add the vinegar and wine and boil rapidly until reduced by half. Stir in the olives, tomatoes and measured water. Reduce the heat and place the lamb shanks on top of the sauce. Cover with a well-fitting lid and cook for *1½–2 hours* until very tender. Baste occasionally and add more water, if necessary. Season to taste with salt and pepper.

3 Meanwhile, make the saffron mash, if serving. Boil the potatoes for about *20 minutes* until just tender. Heat the cream in a small pan, remove from the heat and stir in the saffron. Leave to infuse for *10 minutes*. When the potatoes are cooked, drain well, return to the pan and add the saffron cream and the olive oil. Mash together thoroughly and season with salt and pepper to taste.

4 To serve, divide the saffron mash between 4 plates, top with a lamb shank and spoon over some sauce.

Serves 4

Mexican Beef and Bean Stew

Preparation time: 30 minutes, plus overnight soaking
Cooking time: 2½–3 hours

- 2 tablespoons olive oil
- 750 g/1½ lb boneless shin of beef, cut into 2.5 cm/1 inch cubes
- 1 large onion, chopped
- 2–3 garlic cloves, crushed
- 2 teaspoons ground cumin
- 2 teaspoons ground coriander
- 375 g/12 oz red or black kidney beans, either soaked overnight in water, or canned
- 2–3 large red chillies, roasted, skinned, deseeded and finely chopped
- 2 red peppers, roasted, skinned, deseeded and finely chopped
- 1 bay leaf
- 1 thyme sprig
- 2 large tomatoes, skinned and chopped
- 600 ml/1 pint Beef Stock (see page 9)
- 6 tablespoons chopped fresh coriander
- salt

CORNMEAL DUMPLINGS:

- 65 g/2½ oz plain flour
- 75 g/3 oz fine cornmeal
- 1½ teaspoons caster sugar
- 1 teaspoon baking powder
- ¼ teaspoon salt
- 100 ml/3½ fl oz buttermilk or milk, at room temperature
- 1 egg, beaten
- 25 g/1 oz unsalted butter, melted
- 50 g/2 oz canned sweetcorn kernels, drained

1 Heat the oil in a large heavy-based pan, add the meat, in batches, and fry gently until browned. Remove with a slotted spoon and set aside.

2 Add the onion and garlic to the pan and fry over a low heat until golden, then add the cumin and ground coriander and fry for *1–2 minutes*.

3 Add the drained beans, meat and all the remaining ingredients except the coriander and salt. Pour in just enough water to cover. Bring to the boil. Reduce the heat, cover tightly and simmer over very low heat for *2–2½ hours* until the meat is tender.

4 Meanwhile, make the dumpling mixture. Sift the flour, cornmeal, sugar, baking powder and salt together. Add the buttermilk or milk, egg and butter and mix together, then gently stir in the sweetcorn.

5 About *10–15 minutes* before the end of the cooking time, stir the coriander into the stew and season with salt. Drop tablespoons of the dumpling mixture into the stew, replace the lid and simmer until the dumplings are light and cooked. Serve hot.

Serves 4–6

Pasta and Noodle Dishes

To make pasta in one pot, make the sauce first, set it aside and keep warm, then rinse out the pot, and cook the pasta. You need a large pan for pasta – at least 2 litres/3½ pint capacity – so it doesn't stick together. A pasta pan, fitted with a perforated draining basket, is ideal for cooking large quantities. These are also found in the new, stainless steel multi-pot sets.

Pasta dishes are fast, indeed most of the recipes here take less than 20 minutes to cook. Dried pasta is available in a host of different shapes and colours, and keeps almost indefinitely. Fresh pasta has the advantage of cooking really quickly. Noodles are the oriental equivalent of pasta.

Spaghetti with Chilli Clams

Preparation time: 20 minutes
Cooking time: 20 minutes

- 2 tablespoons olive oil
- 1 small red chilli, deseeded and chopped
- 1 small green chilli, deseeded and chopped
- 3 garlic cloves, chopped
- 125 ml/4 fl oz dry white wine
- 125 ml/4 fl oz Fish Stock (see page 9)
- 50 g/2 oz butter, cut into cubes
- 500 g/1 lb fresh spaghetti
- salt
- 1 kg/2 lb small clams, rinsed

1 Heat the oil in a pan, add the chillies and garlic and cook gently for *2–3 minutes*. Add the wine and stock, and bring to the boil. Lower the heat, whisk in the butter, cover and simmer for *6–7 minutes*. Remove from the heat and keep warm.

2 Rinse the pan, fill it with lightly salted water and bring to the boil. Add the pasta and cook according to packet instructions or until just tender.

3 Drain the pasta and place in a warm bowl. Reheat the wine mixture, add the clams and cook, covered, for *3–4 minutes*. Shake the pan to ensure that the clams cook evenly. Remove and discard any that do not open. Add the clams and their sauce to the pasta, toss to combine and serve immediately.

Serves 6–8

Variation
Spaghetti with Chilli Prawn Sauce

Preparation time: 10 minutes
Cooking time: about 15–20 minutes

1 Cook the pasta following step 2 of the main recipe. Drain and keep warm.

2 Heat 2 tablespoons olive oil and 1 oz butter in the pan and fry the chillies and garlic for *2–3 minutes*. Add 500 g/1 lb cooked peeled prawns and cook for *2 minutes*. Tip the drained pasta back into the pan and toss to mix. Season with salt and pepper to taste and sprinkle generously with chopped flat leaf parsley.

Spaghetti with Tomato and Caper Sauce

Preparation time: 15 minutes
Cooking time: 20 minutes

- 500 g/1 lb passata (Italian sieved tomatoes)
- 1 teaspoon olive oil
- 2 garlic cloves, chopped
- 2 tablespoons capers
- 1 tablespoon balsamic vinegar
- 2 thin slices Parma ham, cut into thin shreds
- 500 g/1 lb spaghetti
- salt

1 Heat the oil in a large heavy-based pan. Add the garlic and tomatoes and cook over a high heat for *5–6 minutes*. Add the capers, balsamic vinegar and ham. Stir to combine. Remove from the pan and keep warm.

2 Rinse the pan, fill it with lightly salted boling water and bring to the boil. Add the pasta and cook according to the packet instructions or until just tender, and drain well. Add the sauce to the spaghetti and toss to combine.

3 Serve the pasta in warm bowls.

Serves 6–8

Cook's Tools

The great advantage of one-pot cooking is the simplicity of the utensils that are required. As all the cooking takes place in a single container there is no need for the usual array of pots and pans. The many functions mean that a number of cooking processes can take place at the same time.

Tagine

Muslin

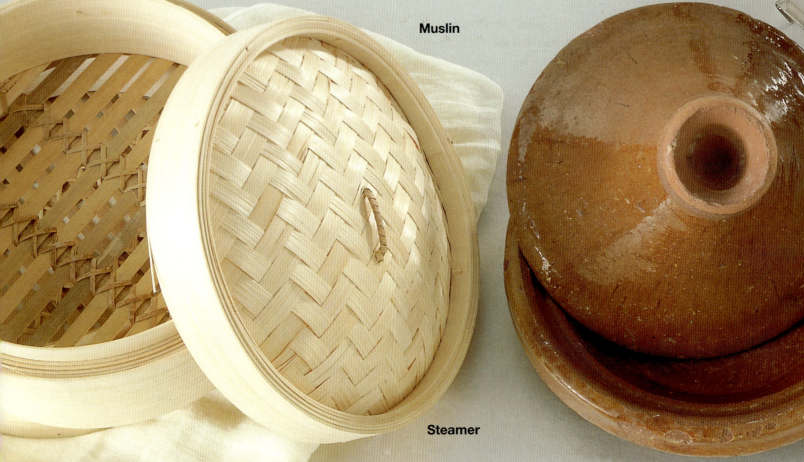

Steamer

Steamers The bamboo steamer has a slatted basket and is used extensively in Chinese cooking. The steamers are stackable so different layers of food can be steamed over one pot of water. Steaming is an ideal method of cooking for many types of food. It is particularly beneficial for vegetables, as the nutritional content of the food is maintained and few vitamins are lost as they are when boiling.

Muslin is used to line steamers when cooking foods which could drop through the holes, such as couscous. It is also used to wrap puddings during steaming.

Tagine This is a round, earthenware pot, used extensively in North African cuisine, in which stews are both cooked and served. It is glazed and has a conical lid that traps steam as it rises and so prevents the stew from drying out. Tagines are available in a number of sizes, the smallest of which is suitable for an individual serving. In restaurants, the tagine is brought to the table so that the food remains hot.

Multi-pot set

Ladle

Ladle This is essential for serving sauces and soups and can also be used to add measured amounts of liquid to soups and stocks. When cooked, ladles can be used to scoop food out of the saucepan or steamer. The best material for a ladle is stainless steel, but they are also available in plastic.

Multi-pot set This is a stacked cooking system that allows you to prepare a number of dishes at the same time. One or all of the sections of the pot can be used and by stacking the sections, food can be boiled and the steam used to cook food in the layers above. The base section is sturdy enough to support the other sections and it is ideal for cooking soups and casseroles as a heavy-based saucepan. It is also good for cooking pasta, which needs plenty of space to move in order to prevent it sticking to the bottom of the saucepan. The pasta is placed in the draining basket which is then placed in the heavy-based saucepan. When cooked, the pasta can easily be drained.

Creamy Mushroom Linguine

Preparation time: 20 minutes
Cooking time: 25 minutes

- 100 g/3½ oz butter
- 200 g/7 oz flat mushrooms, sliced
- 200 g/7 oz brown mushrooms, sliced
- 200 g/7 oz button mushrooms, sliced
- 2 garlic cloves, finely chopped
- 175 ml/6 fl oz dry white wine
- 500 ml/17 fl oz double cream
- 500 g/1 lb fresh linguine or spaghetti
- 1 tablespoon chopped thyme
- salt and pepper

TO GARNISH:

- Parmesan cheese shavings
- thyme sprigs

1 Heat a third of the butter over a medium heat in a large heavy-based pan. Add the flat mushrooms and cook for *1–2 minutes* or until golden brown, then remove. Repeat with the two remaining types of mushroom, adding a third of the butter to the pan each time. Set aside.

2 Add the garlic to the pan and cook for *1 minute*. Add the wine, bring it slowly to the boil and simmer for *5 minutes*. Pour in the cream and stir to combine. Simmer, uncovered, for *10 minutes* or until the mixture thickens, stirring occasionally. Remove from the pan, stir in the mushrooms and keep warm.

3 Rinse the pan, fill it with lightly salted water and bring to the boil. Add the pasta and cook according to packet instructions or until just tender. Drain well and keep warm.

4 Add the mushrooms and wine mixture to the pan with the thyme and cook for *1 minute* until heated through. Season with salt and pepper to taste.

5 Place the pasta in a large warm serving bowl and top with the mushroom sauce. Garnish with Parmesan shavings and thyme sprigs and serve immediately.

Serves 6–8

Pasta with Salmon and Broccoli

Any other pasta shape can be used, as can those coloured with spinach or tomato.
You could also try canned tuna, smoked oysters or mussels instead of the salmon.

Preparation time: 20 minutes
Cooking time: 15 minutes

- 2 tablespoons olive oil
- 1 garlic clove, crushed
- 6 spring onions, chopped
- 1 red pepper, cored, deseeded and diced
- 250 g/8 oz broccoli florets

- 200 g/7 oz can salmon in brine
- 300 ml/½ pint soured cream
- 375 g/12 oz fresh pasta spirals
- salt

1 Heat the olive oil in a large heavy-based pan. Add the garlic, spring onions, red pepper and broccoli and cook for *3–4 minutes*.

2 Add the salmon, including the brine, and the soured cream. Mix well and simmer for *2–3 minutes*. Remove from the pan and keep warm.

3 Rinse the pan, fill it with lightly salted water and bring to the boil. Add the pasta and cook according to packet instructions or until just tender. Drain well then put back in the pan.

4 Add the sauce to the pasta, toss well to mix then place in a warm serving bowl.

Serves 6 as a starter

Fresh Tagliatelle with Porcini

Preparation time: 10 minutes, plus soaking
Cooking time: 25 minutes

- 375–500 g/12 oz–1 lb fresh
  tagliatelle

MUSHROOM SAUCE:

- 25 g/1 oz dried porcini
  mushrooms
- 2 tablespoons olive oil
- 8 large mushrooms, thinly
  sliced

- 3 garlic cloves, finely
  chopped
- 350 ml/12 fl oz Beef or
  Chicken Stock (see page 9)
- 3 egg yolks
- 300 ml/½ pint single cream
- salt and pepper
- Parmesan cheese shavings,
  to serve

1 Place the porcini mushrooms in a bowl, cover with hot water and leave to soak for *20 minutes*. Drain, reserving the liquid. Rinse the porcini to remove any grit.

2 Heat the oil in a large heavy-based pan, add the mushrooms, and fry until lightly browned then remove. Add the garlic and cook for *30 seconds*. Pour in the stock and reserved porcini liquid, then boil until reduced by half. Add the porcini, mushrooms, egg yolks and cream; stir well together. Simmer for *2 minutes* and season to taste. Remove from the pan and keep warm.

3 Rinse the pan, fill it with lightly salted water and bring to the boil. Add the tagliatelle and cook for *2–3 minutes* or until just tender. Drain well and put in a warm serving dish. Pour the sauce over the pasta, mix well and serve on warm plates with Parmesan shavings.

Serves 4

Penne with Tomato, Olives and Rocket

Preparation time: 15 minutes
Cooking time: 12 minutes

- 1 kg/2 lb tomatoes, skinned
- 50 ml/2 fl oz extra virgin olive oil
- 250 g/8 oz feta cheese, cubed
- 125 g/4 oz pitted black olives
- 125 g/4 oz streaky bacon, rinded

- 500 g/1 lb fresh penne
- 1 bunch rocket or young spinach leaves
- salt and pepper

1 Finely chop the tomatoes and place them in a large bowl with their juice. Add the olive oil, feta and olives. Dry-fry the bacon in a large heavy-based pan until crisp, then chop roughly. Add to the tomato mixture.

2 Rinse the pan, fill it with lightly salted water and bring to the boil. Cook the pasta according to packet instructions until it is just tender. Add the rocket or spinach leaves just before draining the pasta thoroughly.

3 Combine the pasta with the tomato mixture and toss gently to combine. Season with salt and pepper to taste and serve immediately.

Serves 4–6

Variation
Penne with Roasted Peppers

Preparation time: 10 minutes
Cooking time: 10 minutes

1 Roast 8 mixed red and yellow peppers under a grill preheated to high for about *5 minutes*, turning several times, until the skins blister and blacken. Allow to cool, then remove the skins and seeds. Slice the flesh into thin strips.

2 Continue as in the main recipe, substituting the pepper strips for the tomatoes.

Penne with Chilli and Cauliflower

Preparation time: 15 minutes
Cooking time: 20 minutes

- 2 teaspoons olive oil
- 2 garlic cloves, finely chopped
- 1–2 small red chillies, sliced lengthways and deseeded
- ½ small cauliflower, cut into small florets
- 125 ml/4 fl oz Chicken Stock (see page 9)
- 125 ml/4 fl oz dry white wine
- 500 g/1lb fresh ribbed penne
- 50 g/2 oz small pitted black olives
- salt

1 Heat the oil in a large, heavy-based pan. Add the garlic and stir until soft and golden. Add the chillies and cook for about *30 seconds*, then remove the garlic and chillies from the pan using a slotted spoon.

2 Add the cauliflower florets, the stock and wine to the pan. Cover and cook for *6–8 minutes* or until the cauliflower is just tender. Remove from the pan and keep warm.

3 Rinse the pan, fill it with lightly salted water and bring to the boil. Add the pasta and cook according to the packet instructions or until just tender. Drain well.

4 Put the pasta into a warm serving bowl. Add the cauliflower florets, garlic, chillies and olives. Toss to combine.

Serves 6–8

Variation
Penne with Chilli and Broccoli

Preparation time: 15 minutes
Cooking time: 20 minutes

1 Bring a pan of lightly salted water to the boil. Add 500 g/1 lb broccoli florets, return to the boil, then cook, uncovered, for *3 minutes* until just tender. Drain and break into smaller pieces. Dice the stalks.

2 Cook the pasta, drain, reserving a little of the water, and transfer to a warm serving dish.

3 Add the broccoli florets and stalks with salt, pepper and chopped fresh chilli or dried chilli flakes to taste. Stir in 50 g/2 oz each butter and freshly grated Parmesan cheese. Mix well, adding a little of the reserved pasta water if the mixture is too dry. Serve with extra Parmesan.

Fettuccine with Sun-dried Tomato Sauce

If you cannot find a jar of ready-prepared roasted peppers, then roast some yourself. Put 1 red and 1 yellow pepper under a preheated hot grill until their skins are charred, turning them frequently. Remove them from the heat and put them into a polythene bag (this makes it easier to remove the skins). When the peppers are cool enough to handle, peel off the skins. Cut the peppers in half, remove the cores and seeds and cut the flesh into thin strips.

Preparation time: 10 minutes
Cooking time: 10 minutes

- 6 bacon rashers, rinded and
  cut into thin strips
- 250 g/8 oz fresh tri-colour
  fettuccine
- 175 g/6 oz jar red pesto
  sauce
- 250 g/8 oz jar roasted mixed
  peppers in oil, drained
- 150 ml/¼ pint double cream,
  to serve

1 Place the bacon in a large heavy-based pan and dry-fry over a medium heat until very crisp. Remove and set aside.

2 Fill a pan with lightly salted water and bring to the boil. Add the pasta and cook according to packet instructions or until just tender. Remove from the pan, drain and keep warm.

3 Pour the red pesto sauce and the roasted peppers in oil into the pan and heat through. Mix the pasta and sauce together. Serve on warm plates, topped with the bacon strips and a spoonful of cream.

Serves 4

Variation
Fettuccine with Spicy Salami

Preparation time: 10 minutes
Cooking time: 10 minutes

Make the sauce as in the main recipe, but instead of bacon use 8 slices of salami chopped into thin strips. When heating the prepared sauce, add 2 tablespoons of chilli sauce. You can use a deseeded and finely chopped fresh red chilli instead, but heat for a little longer to ensure that it is tender.

Noodles in Spicy Broth

Preparation time: 15 minutes
Cooking time: 15 minutes

- 250 g/8 oz cooked peeled
  prawns
- 1 teaspoon cornflour
- 375 g/12 oz egg noodles
- 600 ml/1 pint Chicken Stock
  (see page 9)
- 2 tablespoons light soy
  sauce
- 3 tablespoons vegetable oil
- 2 spring onions, thinly
  shredded

- 125 g/4 oz bamboo shoots or
  button mushrooms, thinly
  sliced
- 125 g/4 oz spinach leaves or
  Chinese leaves, thinly sliced
- 2 tablespoons dry sherry
- 1–2 teaspoons sesame oil
- salt

TO GARNISH:

- 1 red chilli, chopped
- coriander sprigs

1 Put the prawns in a bowl with a pinch of salt. Mix the cornflour to a smooth paste with 1 tablespoon cold water, and stir into the prawns.

2 Fill a large saucepan with lightly salted water and bring to the boil. Add the egg noodles and cook according to the packet instructions until just tender. Drain well and place the noodles in a large, warm serving bowl. Bring the stock to the boil and pour it over the noodles with half of the soy sauce. Keep warm.

3 Heat the oil in the pan and add the shredded spring onions to flavour the oil. Add the prawn mixture and the shredded bamboo shoots or mushrooms and spinach or Chinese leaves. Stir a few times, and then add 1½ teaspoons salt, the remaining soy sauce and the sherry. Cook for *1–2 minutes*, stirring constantly.

4 Pour the mixture over the noodles and sprinkle with sesame oil. Serve garnished with chopped red chilli and coriander sprigs.

Serves 4

Rice and Couscous

Savoury rice dishes come mainly from Asia, but creamy risottos, made with arborio rice, are an Italian speciality. Couscous is a form of pasta, made from fine grains of semolina, and comes from North Africa, where it accompanies spicy aromatic stews made with lamb or chicken and vegetables. In North Africa couscous is often cooked in a couscoussier, a special pot that sits over the stew. Here you can use a large steamer such as the steamer section of a multi-pot, but it will need lining with muslin.

Chicken Stew with Couscous

Preparation time: 30 minutes
Cooking time: 1½ hours

- **4 tablespoons olive oil**
- **2 onions, chopped**
- **1 green or yellow pepper, cored, deseeded and chopped**
- **3 tomatoes, skinned and chopped**
- **2 red chillies, deseeded and finely chopped**
- **375 g/12 oz turnips, quartered**
- **250 g/8 oz small carrots, quartered**
- **3 courgettes, sliced**
- **125 g/4 oz fine green beans, topped and tailed**
- **1 teaspoon ground coriander**
- **1 teaspoon cumin**
- **1.5 kg/3 lb chicken, jointed**
- **600 ml/1 pint hot water**
- **250 g/8 oz cooked or canned chickpeas**
- **375 g/12 oz couscous**
- **25 g/1 oz butter, diced**
- **salt and pepper**

HOT SAUCE:
- **2 tablespoons tomato purée**
- **½–1 teaspoon Harissa Paste (see page 8)**

1 Heat the olive oil in a large heavy-based pan over a medium heat and fry the onions, pepper, tomatoes and chillies for *5–6 minutes* until soft. Add the turnips, carrots, courgettes and beans and stir well. Add the spices, salt and pepper to taste, chicken pieces and measured hot water. Simmer gently for *20 minutes*.

2 Add the chickpeas to the chicken mixture and simmer for *25–30 minutes*.

3 Meanwhile, soak the couscous in a bowl of cold water for *10–15 minutes* then stir gently with a wooden spoon to break up any lumps. Drain in a colander. Line a steamer with some muslin and tip in the couscous.

4 Put the steamer containing the couscous over the pan with the chicken (it should not touch the stew below) and steam gently for about *15–20 minutes*. Season the couscous to taste and gently break up any lumps. Dot with butter.

5 To make the hot sauce, take a couple of ladlefuls of liquid from the chicken stew and mix with the tomato purée and harissa. Serve the stew with the couscous and add the hot sauce separately.

Serves 4–6

Variation
Chicken with Green Couscous

Preparation time: 15 minutes

1 Whisk together 150 ml/¼ pint olive oil and 4 tablespoons lemon juice. Season with salt and pepper. Finely chop a bunch of spring onions and 50 g/2 oz rocket or watercress. Deseed and finely chop ½ cucumber. Tip the cooked couscous into a warm dish and pour over the oil and lemon mixture and the chopped vegetables. Mix thoroughly and serve immediately with the chicken stew.

Lamb with Couscous

Preparation time: 30 minutes
Cooking time: about 1 hour

- 500 g/1 lb lean lamb, cut into
  large cubes
- 900 ml/1½ pints water
- 2 onions, quartered and
  thickly sliced
- 2 garlic cloves, crushed
- pinch of saffron threads,
  crushed
- 1 teaspoon ground cinnamon
- ½ teaspoon paprika
- 1 red chilli, deseeded and
  finely chopped
- ½ teaspoon ground ginger
- 250 g/8 oz small carrots,
  quartered lengthways
- 250 g/8 oz small turnips,
  quartered
- 250 g/8 oz kohlrabi or
  celeriac, cut into large
  chunks
- 500 g/1 lb couscous
- 250 g/8 oz courgettes,
  quartered lengthways
- 250 g/8 oz broad beans
- 4 tomatoes, quartered
- large bunch of coriander,
  chopped
- large bunch of flat leaf
  parsley, chopped
- 40 g/1½ oz unsalted butter
- salt and pepper

1 Put the lamb into a large heavy-based pan. Add the measured water, the onions, garlic, saffron, cinnamon, paprika, chilli, ginger and salt and pepper to taste. Bring to the boil, remove any scum from the surface, cover and simmer very gently for about *30 minutes*.

2 Meanwhile, soak the couscous in a bowl of cold water for *10–15 minutes* then stir gently with a wooden spoon to break up any lumps. Drain in a colander. Line a steamer with some muslin and tip in the couscous.

3 Add the carrots, turnips and kohlrabi or celeriac to the lamb. Put the steamer containing the couscous over the pan with the lamb (it should not touch the stew below) and steam gently for *10 minutes*.

4 Add the courgettes, broad beans, tomatoes, coriander and parsley to the lamb and cook for a further *5–10 minutes* or until the vegetables, lamb and couscous are tender.

5 Fork through the couscous to separate the grains, then turn on to a large warm serving plate. Dot the butter over the top, stir in and season with salt and pepper. Form into a mound with a large well in the centre and place the lamb in the well. Using a slotted spoon, lift the vegetables from the cooking broth and place on and around the lamb. Serve the remaining broth in a separate warm bowl.

Serves 4

Ingredients

The one pot is so versatile and can be used to cook so many different types of food, from soups to puddings, that ingredients are many and varied. A good selection of fresh herbs and spices is essential for soups and casseroles, as are stocks and a variety of rice and pulses.

Lemon Thyme

Flat leaf parsley

Rosemary

Flat leaf parsley can be used in a wide range of dishes, from soups to fish. It has a stronger flavour than the curly variety and is available all year.
Lemon thyme is a tiny-leafed herb ideal for stuffings. To ensure a year round supply, home-dried or frozen lemon thyme is a better option than dried or powdered thyme.
Rosemary has a pungent, flavour, and an affinity with lamb, but is also good with chicken, veal and rabbit.
Arborio rice has medium, roundish grains that absorb a lot of liquid without becoming soft. It is ideal not only for risottos, but also for any dish requiring long, gentle cooking.
Long- grain rice is available in many varieties. During cooking, the grains remain separate, making it ideal for salads, stuffings and as an accompaniment.

Couscous is a cereal made from hard wheat semolina. It is steamed and often flavoured with butter and herbs. It can be served as a side dish, similar to rice.
Chicken stock is made by simmering chicken with vegetables and herbs. An

Arborio rice

Long-grain rice

Couscous

Chicken stock

Harissa paste

Fish stock

Ground coriander

Saffron threads

Ground cinnamon

Turmeric

ideal base for casseroles and soups, it can be home-made (see page 9) or bought fresh.
Harissa paste (see page 8) is made from chillies and olive oil and is used as a marinade or served with couscous.
Fish stock (see page 9) can be made using most fish, but

those with stronger flavours are best. Oily varieties, such as salmon, should be avoided. It is often used in sauces served with fish.
Ground coriander can be used on its own, or mixed with other spices to flavour dishes. The flavour is enhanced if the

seeds are toasted before being crushed.
Saffron threads are picked by hand, making it an expensive spice . It is used to colour rice, and to flavour fish and vegetable soups.
Ground cinnamon is often used in baking. With its

distinctive flavour, it is used in a wide range of sweet dishes and is especially good with apples and chocolate.
Turmeric has a harsh, earthy flavour, and a vibrant yellow colour. It is often used as a substitute for saffron due to its low price and wide availability.

Lamb with Couscous

Preparation time: 30 minutes
Cooking time: about 1 hour

- 500 g/1 lb lean lamb, cut into large cubes
- 900 ml/1½ pints water
- 2 onions, quartered and thickly sliced
- 2 garlic cloves, crushed
- pinch of saffron threads, crushed
- 1 teaspoon ground cinnamon
- ½ teaspoon paprika
- 1 red chilli, deseeded and finely chopped
- ½ teaspoon ground ginger
- 250 g/8 oz small carrots, quartered lengthways
- 250 g/8 oz small turnips, quartered
- 250 g/8 oz kohlrabi or celeriac, cut into large chunks
- 500 g/1 lb couscous
- 250 g/8 oz courgettes, quartered lengthways
- 250 g/8 oz broad beans
- 4 tomatoes, quartered
- large bunch of coriander, chopped
- large bunch of flat leaf parsley, chopped
- 40 g/1½ oz unsalted butter
- salt and pepper

1 Put the lamb into a large heavy-based pan. Add the measured water, the onions, garlic, saffron, cinnamon, paprika, chilli, ginger and salt and pepper to taste. Bring to the boil, remove any scum from the surface, cover and simmer very gently for about *30 minutes*.

2 Meanwhile, soak the couscous in a bowl of cold water for *10–15 minutes* then stir gently with a wooden spoon to break up any lumps. Drain in a colander. Line a steamer with some muslin and tip in the couscous.

3 Add the carrots, turnips and kohlrabi or celeriac to the lamb. Put the steamer containing the couscous over the pan with the lamb (it should not touch the stew below) and steam gently for *10 minutes*.

4 Add the courgettes, broad beans, tomatoes, coriander and parsley to the lamb and cook for a further *5–10 minutes* or until the vegetables, lamb and couscous are tender.

5 Fork through the couscous to separate the grains, then turn on to a large warm serving plate. Dot the butter over the top, stir in and season with salt and pepper. Form into a mound with a large well in the centre and place the lamb in the well. Using a slotted spoon, lift the vegetables from the cooking broth and place on and around the lamb. Serve the remaining broth in a separate warm bowl.

Serves 4

North African Fish Stew with Couscous

Preparation time: 30–45 minutes
Cooking time: 45 minutes

- 4 tablespoons olive oil
- 2 onions, cut into small wedges, but still attached to the root
- 1–2 garlic cloves, chopped
- 1 celery stick, sliced
- 1 red or green pepper, cored, deseeded and cut into strips
- 1 teaspoon Harissa Paste (see page 8)
- 1 teaspoon ground cumin
- 500 g/1 lb couscous
- 400 g/13 oz can chopped tomatoes
- 1 tablespoon tomato purée
- 2 carrots, sliced
- large pinch of saffron threads
- 1.2 litres/2 pints Fish or Chicken Stock (see page 9)
- 125 g/4 oz canned chickpeas, drained
- 40 g/1½ oz unsalted butter
- 1–1.25 kg/2–2½ lb firm white fish (bass, mullet, bream, snapper, cod), scaled, gutted and cut into large pieces
- 1½ tablespoons chopped flat leaf parsley
- 1½ tablespoons chopped coriander
- salt and pepper
- coriander sprigs, to garnish

1 Heat the oil in a large heavy-based pan, add the onions, garlic and celery and cook for *10–12 minutes* until soft. Add the pepper, harissa and cumin and fry for *5 minutes*.

2 Meanwhile, soak the couscous in a bowl of cold water for *10–15 minutes* then stir gently with a wooden spoon to break up any lumps. Drain in a colander. Line a steamer with some muslin and tip in the couscous.

3 Add the tomatoes, tomato purée, carrots, saffron, stock and chickpeas to the onion mixture. Put the steamer with the couscous over the pan with the vegetables (it should not touch the stew below) and bring to the boil. Reduce the heat and simmer for *15 minutes*. Season to taste.

4 Fork through the couscous to separate the grains, then turn on to a large warm serving plate. Dot the butter over the top, stir in and season with salt and pepper. Form into a mound with a large well in the centre and keep warm. Add the fish pieces to the stew and cook for *5 minutes* or until they are white and starting to flake. Stir in the parsley and coriander. Serve the stew spooned over the couscous and garnished with coriander sprigs.

Serves 4–6

Green Lentil and Vegetable Tagine with Couscous

Preparation time: 45 minutes
Cooking time: about 1 hour

- 125 g/4 oz green lentils, rinsed
- 600 ml/1 pint water
- 4 tablespoons extra virgin olive oil
- 2 small onions, cut into wedges
- 2 garlic cloves, chopped
- 1 tablespoon ground coriander
- 2 teaspoons ground cumin
- 1 teaspoon ground turmeric
- 1 teaspoon ground cinnamon

- 12 new potatoes, halved if large
- 2 large carrots, thickly sliced
- 250 g/8 oz couscous
- 2 courgettes, sliced
- 175 g/6 oz button mushrooms
- 300 ml/½ pint tomato juice
- 1 tablespoon tomato purée
- 125 g/4 oz ready-to-eat dried apricots, chopped
- 2 tablespoons chilli sauce, plus extra to serve (optional)

1 Put the lentils in a large heavy-based pan with the measured water. Bring to the boil, cover and simmer for *20 minutes*. Remove the lentils and their cooking liquid and set aside.

2 Heat half of the oil in the pan and fry the onions, garlic and spices for *5 minutes*. Add the potatoes and sliced carrots and fry for a further *5 minutes*. Add the lentils with their cooking liquid, cover and simmer gently for *15 minutes*. Remove the lentil mixture from the pan and set aside.

3 Meanwhile, soak the couscous in a bowl of cold water for *10–15 minutes* then stir gently with a wooden spoon to break up any lumps. Drain in a colander. Line a steamer with some muslin and tip in the couscous.

4 Heat the remaining oil in the pan and fry the courgettes and mushrooms for *4–5 minutes* until golden. Return the lentil mixture to the pan with the tomato juice, tomato purée, apricots and chilli sauce and bring back to the boil. Put the steamer with the couscous over the pan (it should not touch the stew below) and cook for *10–15 minutes* until the vegetables and lentils are tender and the couscous is cooked.

5 Pile the couscous on to a large warm serving plate and spoon on the vegetable and lentil tagine. Serve the juices separately, with extra chilli sauce, if liked.

Serves 4–6

Tomato and Mushroom Risotto

Preparation time: 10 minutes
Cooking time: 35 minutes

- 75 g/3 oz unsalted butter
- 1 onion, finely chopped
- 250 g/8 oz mushrooms, sliced
- 3 large tomatoes, skinned and finely chopped
- 400 g/13 oz arborio rice
- 1 litre/1¾ pints hot Chicken Stock (see page 9)
- 40 g/1½ oz Parmesan cheese, grated
- salt and pepper
- thyme sprigs, to garnish

1 Heat three-quarters of the butter in a large heavy-based pan. Add the onion and cook gently, stirring, over a low heat for *5 minutes*. Add the mushrooms and three-quarters of the tomatoes and continue to stir over a low heat for a further *5 minutes*.

2 Add the rice and stir to coat with the butter. Increase the heat and cook, stirring constantly, for a further *30 seconds*. Pour in a ladleful of the hot stock. Reduce the heat to low and stir until the stock is absorbed. Continue adding the stock, a ladleful at a time, stirring constantly and adding more only when the previous addition has been absorbed. The risotto is ready when all the stock has been absorbed and the grains of rice are tender but still firm. This will take about *25 minutes*.

3 Stir in the remaining butter with the Parmesan and cook until the cheese has melted. Season to taste with salt and pepper, transfer to warm bowls and serve immediately, sprinkled with the remaining tomatoes and garnished with sprigs of thyme.

Serves 4

Seafood Risotto

Preparation time: 15 minutes
Cooking time: 45 minutes

- 1 kg/2 lb mixed seafood (octopus, squid, prawns, white fish)
- 2 tablespoons olive oil
- 1 large onion, chopped
- 2 garlic cloves, crushed
- 250 g/8 oz arborio rice
- 600–750 ml/1–1¼ pints Fish Stock (see page 9)
- 3 tomatoes, skinned and chopped
- 2 tablespoons finely chopped flat leaf parsley
- salt and pepper

TO SERVE:

- 4 red or green chillies
- lime wedges

1 To prepare the seafood, wash and clean the octopus or squid and slice them into rings. Cut the tentacles into small pieces. Wash and peel the prawns. Cut the fish into large chunks.

2 Heat the oil in a large heavy-based pan and fry the onion and garlic gently until soft and golden. Add the rice and stir for *1–2 minutes*.

3 Add some of the stock and the chopped tomatoes and bring to the boil. Reduce the heat and simmer gently, stirring in more stock as and when necessary, until all the liquid has been absorbed and the rice is tender. After *15 minutes*, add the prepared seafood. Stir in the parsley and season with salt and pepper when the rice is cooked.

4 Cut the chillies into thin strips and use as a garnish. Serve the risotto with lime wedges.

Serves 4

Chicken and Broccoli Risotto

Preparation time: 15 minutes
Cooking time: 30–35 minutes

- 40 g/1½ oz butter
- 2 tablespoons olive oil
- 2 boneless, skinless chicken breasts, diced
- ½ onion, very finely chopped
- 1 garlic clove, finely chopped
- 1–2 red chillies, deseeded and very finely chopped (optional)
- 300 g/10 oz arborio rice
- 1 litre/1¾ pints hot Chicken Stock (see page 9)
- 250 g/8 oz broccoli florets, cooked
- 3 tablespoons grated Parmesan cheese
- salt and pepper

1 Heat 15 g/½ oz of the butter with the oil in a large heavy-based pan, add the diced chicken and stir-fry gently for *2–3 minutes*. Add the onion and fry for *5 minutes* until it is soft but not coloured. Add the garlic and chilli, if using, and fry until the garlic is golden but not browned.

2 Add the rice to the pan and stir for *1–2 minutes*. Add the hot stock, a ladleful at a time, stirring constantly and allowing the liquid to be absorbed before adding more. The process will take about *25 minutes*, leaving the rice tender but still firm.

3 Add the broccoli florets to the rice with the Parmesan. Season with salt and pepper and stir in the remaining butter.

Serves 4

Variation
Chicken Liver and Mushroom Risotto

1 Finely chop 250 g/8 oz chicken livers. Heat 15 g/½ oz butter and 2 tablespoons oil in a large heavy-based pan, add the chicken livers and stir-fry gently for *2–3 minutes*. Add ½ very finely chopped onion and stir-fry for *5 minutes* until soft. Add 1 finely chopped garlic clove and fry until it is golden.

2 Add 300 g/10 oz arborio rice and stir for *1–2 minutes*. Gradually add 1 litre/1¾ pints hot stock, as in the main recipe, then 125 g/4 oz mushrooms, briefly cooked in a little butter, with 3 tablespoons grated Parmesan. Season with salt and pepper and stir in 25 g/1 oz butter.

Kedgeree

This Anglo-Indian dish was originally served for breakfast, but also makes a good light lunch or supper. It is good served with chutney or tomato relish.

Preparation time: 10 minutes
Cooking time: 15–20 minutes

- 500 g/1 lb smoked haddock fillets
- milk, for poaching
- 50 g/2 oz butter
- 1 small onion or 2–3 spring onions, finely chopped
- 250 g/8 oz long-grain rice, cooked according to packet instructions
- 4 hard-boiled eggs, chopped
- 4 tablespoons finely chopped flat leaf parsley
- salt and pepper

TO GARNISH:
- spring onion tassels (see page 8)
- hard-boiled egg wedges

1 Place the haddock in a large heavy-based pan and add enough milk to cover. Simmer gently for *10–15 minutes*. Lift off and discard the skin and flake the fish. Reserve the milk.

2 Heat the butter in the pan, add the onion or spring onions and cook gently until soft but not coloured. Add the rice and stir to heat it through.

3 Add the flaked haddock, taking care not to break up the flesh too much. Gently stir in the parsley and the reserved milk, then add the chopped hard-boiled eggs. Season to taste with salt and pepper and turn into a shallow warm serving dish.

4 Garnish with spring onion tassels and wedges of hard-boiled egg.

Serves 4

Classic Paella

Preparation time: about 40 minutes
Cooking time: about 1¼ hours

- 1 kg/2 lb fresh mussels
- 4 garlic cloves
- 1 bunch of fresh mixed herbs
- 150 ml/¼ pint dry white wine
- 2 litres/3½ pints hot Chicken Stock (see page 9) or water
- 4 small squid, cleaned and sliced into rings
- 4 tablespoons virgin olive oil
- 1 large onion, finely chopped
- 1 red pepper, cored, deseeded and chopped
- 4 large ripe tomatoes, skinned, deseeded and chopped
- 12 skinned and boned chicken thighs, cut into bite-sized pieces
- 500 g/1 lb arborio rice
- 125 g/4 oz fresh or frozen peas
- 12 large raw prawns, peeled (optional)
- salt and pepper

TO GARNISH:

- 1 tablespoon chopped flat leaf parsley
- parsley sprigs

1 Scrub the mussels with a stiff brush and scrape off the beards and barnacles with a small sharp knife. Discard any open mussels.

2 Slice 2 garlic cloves and crush the rest. Put the slices in a large heavy-based pan with the herbs, wine, 150 ml/¼ pint stock or water and season with salt and pepper to taste. Add the mussels, cover the pan tightly and bring to the boil. Shake the pan and simmer for *5 minutes* until the mussels open. Remove the mussels from the liquid and set aside, discarding any which remain closed. Strain the liquid and reserve.

3 Fry the squid in half the oil for *5 minutes*, stirring frequently.

4 Add the onion, red pepper and crushed garlic and cook gently, stirring frequently, for *5 minutes* until softened. Add the mussel cooking liquid and tomatoes and season. Bring to the boil, then simmer over a gentle heat, stirring, for *15–20 minutes* until the mixture is thick. Transfer to a bowl.

5 Sauté the chicken in the remaining oil for *5 minutes*. Add the rice and turn it in the oil for *3 minutes*. Stir the squid mixture into the pan. Add about one-third of the remaining stock and bring to the boil, stirring constantly.

6 Boil rapidly for *3–4 minutes*. Cover the pan and simmer for *30 minutes*. Add more stock as the rice becomes dry and stir frequently, moving the rice into the centre so that it cooks evenly. The paella is ready when the chicken is cooked, the rice is tender but still firm and almost all the liquid has been absorbed.

7 Check the seasoning, add the peas and prawns, if using, and simmer, stirring, for *5 minutes* or until cooked, adding stock or water if required.

8 Arrange the mussels decoratively on top of the paella, cover the pan tightly with kitchen foil and cook for *5 minutes* or until the mussels are hot. Serve the paella in warm individual bowls, sprinkled with parsley and garnished with parsley sprigs.

Serves 6

Variation
Paella with Rabbit

- 4 tablespoons olive oil
- 1 kg/2 lb chicken, cut into small pieces
- 4 small rabbit portions
- 2 Spanish onions, chopped
- 4 cloves of garlic, chopped
- 1 tablespoon paprika
- 375 g/12 oz arborio rice
- 3 large sun-ripened tomatoes, skinned, deseeded and chopped
- 1.8 litres/3 pints hot Chicken Stock (see page 9)
- 1 rosemary sprig
- large pinch of saffron threads, crushed
- 150 g/5 oz green beans, cut into short lengths
- 125 g/4 oz broad beans
- salt and pepper

1 Heat the oil in a wide casserole. Add the chicken and rabbit, cook until lightly browned. Stir in the onion and garlic. Fry for *5 minutes*, stir in the paprika followed by the rice.

2 Stir for *2–3 minutes*, then stir in the tomatoes with all but 2 tablespoons of the chicken stock, rosemary and salt and pepper. Dissolve the saffron in the reserved 2 tablespoons of stock, then add to the paella and boil for *8–10 minutes* without stirring.

3 Scatter the green beans and broad beans over the paella – do not stir. Gradually turn down the heat and simmer until the rice is tender and the liquid absorbed, this should take about *8–10 minutes*. Cover the paella with a thick cloth, remove from the heat and set aside for *5–10 minutes* before serving.

Puddings and Desserts

Featherlight sponge puddings drenched in sweet sauce are so delicious they have never entirely gone out of favour, even in these calorie-conscious days. They serve equally well for family meals and entertaining, as cooking times can be quite elastic. Completely different but equally delightful are Thai steamed puddings, made with coconut milk and decorated with tropical fruit.

To cook these puddings you need a lidded steamer deep enough to take the pudding bowl. Alternatively set the bowl on a trivet or upturned saucer in the bottom of a large deep saucepan.

Lemon Pudding

Preparation time: 20–30 minutes
Cooking time: 1¾ hours

- 75 g/3 oz butter, softened
  plus extra for greasing
- 125 g/4 oz caster sugar
- 2 eggs, lightly beaten
- 2 tablespoons lemon
  marmalade
- 175 g/6 oz self-raising flour
- 75 ml/3 fl oz milk

SAUCE:
- 125 g/4 oz lemon marmalade
- 2 tablespoons sugar
- 250 ml/8 fl oz water
- 3 teaspoons grated lemon
  rind

1 To make the pudding, beat the butter and sugar in a bowl until the mixture is light and fluffy and holds the trail of the beaters. Beat in the eggs and marmalade. Sift in the flour and add enough milk to make a mixture just soft enough to pour.

2 Grease a 1.5 litre/2½ pint pudding bowl and pour in the sponge mixture. Clip on the lid or cover with kitchen foil. Place in a steamer and set over a large pan of simmering water. Cover and cook for *1½ hours*. Remove the pudding from the steamer.

3 To make the sauce, simmer the marmalade, sugar, water and rind in the pan for *10 minutes* or until thickened.

4 Turn the pudding on to a serving plate and serve with the hot sauce.

Serves 4

All-in-one Ginger Pudding

Preparation time: 10 minutes
Cooking time: 1 hour

- 175 g/6 oz self-raising flour
- 150 g/5 oz caster sugar
- 2 teaspoons ground ginger
- 125 g/4 oz butter, melted
- 125 ml/4 fl oz milk

- 1 egg
- 100 g/3½ oz stem ginger, chopped
- 4 tablespoons golden syrup
- cream or ice cream, to serve

1 Grease a 1.5 litre/2½ pint pudding bowl. Sift the flour into a mixing bowl. Add the sugar and ground ginger, and stir well to combine.

2 Make a well in the centre of the mixture. Combine the butter, milk and egg and pour them into the well. Using a wooden spoon or metal whisk, stir to mix. Beat the mixture for *2–3 minutes*, or until it is just combined.

3 Place the chopped stem ginger in the base of the pudding bowl. Top with golden syrup, then spoon the pudding mixture into the bowl. Clip on the lid or cover with kitchen foil. Place the bowl in a steamer and set over a large pan of simmering water. Cover and cook for *1 hour*.

4 To serve, turn the pudding bowl upside down on a serving plate. Tap the top and edges of the bowl and allow the pudding to drop on to the plate. The sauce will trickle over the outside of the pudding. Serve with cream or ice cream.

Serves 8

Rice with Coconut Milk

This Thai dessert is decorated with dry-fried sesame seeds, which provide a delicious crunchy contrast to the soft textures of the rice and mango. To dry-fry sesame seeds, put them in a wok or small frying pan over a gentle heat and toast for *3–4 minutes*, stirring constantly, until golden. Dry-fried sesame can be stored in an air-tight container for *3–4 days*.

Preparation time: 10–15 minutes, plus soaking and standing
Cooking time: 45 minutes–1 hour

- 500 g/1 lb glutinous rice
- 400 ml/13 fl oz canned
  coconut milk
- 175 g/6 oz sugar
- 1 tablespoon salt

TO SERVE:
- 1 sliced mango
- 2 tablespoons dry-fried
  sesame seeds

1 Wash the glutinous rice, cover with water and soak for at least *3 hours*. Drain thoroughly and spread out in a large steamer. Place over a large pan of simmering water and steam for *30–40 minutes*.

2 Combine the coconut milk, sugar and salt in a large pan and bring to the boil over a medium heat, stirring constantly. When it boils, stir in the cooked rice, remove from the heat and cover the pan. Leave to stand for *15 minutes*.

3 Serve with mango slices and sprinkled with the toasted sesame seeds.

Serves 6

Coconut Milk Custards

These individual custards come from Thailand, where they are decorated with exotic flowers. You can use home-grown flowers like nasturtiums and pansies, which are just as pretty and also edible.

Preparation time: 10 minutes
Cooking time: 30 minutes

CUSTARD:
- 250 ml/8 fl oz canned coconut milk
- 175 g/6 oz demerara sugar
- 100 g/3½ oz caster sugar
- 1 teaspoon vanilla essence

TO DECORATE:
- 1 tablespoon desiccated coconut
- edible flowers
- thin slices of fresh coconut (optional)

1 Combine all the ingredients in a mixing bowl and beat well with a hand-held electric mixer or wire whisk.

2 Divide the mixture between four 250 ml/8 fl oz heat-resistant bowls and place them in a steamer. Set over a large pan of simmering water.

3 Steam the custards for *30 minutes*. To test whether they are done, spear one with the tip of a sharp-pointed knife. If it comes out clean, the custards are cooked.

4 Turn the coconut milk custards out of the bowls, sprinkle with desiccated coconut and decorate with flowers. Add some slices of coconut if liked. Serve warm or cold.

Serves 4

Variation
Crunchy Coconut Milk Custards

To add extra texture to the custards, you could stir some pumpkin seeds, lotus seeds or sliced coconut into the basic mixture before steaming.

Steamed Chocolate Sponge

Preparation time: 30 minutes
Cooking time: about 1½ hours

- 125 g/4 oz butter, softened
- 125 g/4 oz caster sugar
- 2 eggs, beaten
- 150 g/5 oz self-raising flour
- 20 g/¾ oz cocoa powder
  mixed with 2 tablespoons
  milk

CHOCOLATE SAUCE:

- 25 g/1 oz butter
- 125 g/4 oz plain chocolate,
  broken into squares
- 2 tablespoons double cream

1 Grease a 900 ml/1½ pint pudding bowl.

2 Place the butter and sugar in a bowl and beat together until the mixture is light and fluffy and holds the trail of the beaters. Gradually add the eggs, beating well between each addition. Sift the flour and fold it in, using a figure-of-eight motion, until thoroughly mixed. Stir in the cocoa powder and milk mixture.

3 Spoon the sponge mixture into the pudding bowl. Clip on the lid or cover with kitchen foil.

4 Place the bowl in a steamer and set over a large pan of simmering water. Steam for about *1½ hours*. Remove the bowl from the steamer.

5 To make the chocolate sauce, put the butter and chocolate in a heatproof bowl and place in the steamer. When the chocolate has melted, beat in the double cream. Serve immediately or keep warm over a very low heat.

6 To serve, turn the pudding out on to a warm serving dish. Pour a little hot chocolate sauce over the top and serve the rest separately.

Serves 4–6

Variation

Steamed Chocolate Sponge with Mocha Sauce

Preparation time: 5 minutes
Cooking time: 10–15 minutes

Make the pudding as in the main recipe and, when it is ready, make a mocha sauce instead of a chocolate one. Melt 25 g/1 oz butter over a low heat, add 25 g/1 oz plain flour and cook for 2 minutes, stirring. Add 600 ml/1 pint milk and bring to the boil. Reduce the heat, add 50 g/2 oz caster sugar and 1 tablespoon each cocoa powder and instant coffee. Cook until these have dissolved. Serve hot.

Poached Figs with Cassis in Cinnamon Sauce

Preparation time: 10 minutes, plus chilling
Cooking time: 10 minutes

- 300 ml/½ pint red wine
- 150 ml/¼ pint cassis
- 2 cinnamon sticks
- 2 strips lemon rind
- 2 strips orange rind
- 300 ml/½ pint water
- 12 large ripe firm figs, washed

SAUCE:
- 150 g/5 oz Greek yogurt
- 2 tablespoons Greek honey
- 1 teaspoon ground cinnamon

1 Place the wine, cassis, cinnamon sticks, citrus rind and water in a saucepan and bring to the boil.

2 Add the figs, cover the pan and simmer gently for *10 minutes* until the figs are dark red and softened. Do not over-cook or the figs will fall apart.

3 Remove the figs with a slotted spoon and place in a serving dish. Bring the poaching liquid to a rolling boil and simmer until it is reduced by half and is thick and syrupy. Pour over the figs and leave to cool.

4 Meanwhile, combine all the sauce ingredients together and set aside to allow the flavours to develop. Serve the figs at room temperature with a spoonful of sauce for each serving.

Serves 4

Tipsy Fruit

Preparation time: 15 minutes
Cooking time: 15 minutes

- 450 ml/¾ pint sweet white
  wine
- 12 large prunes
- 12 dried figs
- 8 dried apple rings
- 8 dried apricots

APRICOT CHEESE:

- 250 g/8 oz dried apricots
- 1 cinnamon stick
- 150 ml/¼ pint orange juice
- 125 g/4 oz fromage frais
- pared rind of ½ orange, cut
  into thin strips

1 Pour the wine into a pan and boil to reduce by half. Place in a large heatproof bowl with the fruit and cover with a piece of kitchen foil or the lid. Put in a steamer and set over a large pan of boiling water. Steam for *15 minutes*.

2 Meanwhile, make the apricot cheese. Place the apricots, cinnamon stick and orange juice in cupped kitchen foil, then seal the edges together carefully. Place in the steamer with the other fruit and steam for *10 minutes*.

3 Remove the cinnamon stick. Put the apricots and orange juice, with the fromage frais, in a food processor or blender and work until smooth. Blanch the orange peel strips in the base of the steamer for *20 seconds*. Cool in cold water.

4 Make a bed of apricot cheese on each of 4 plates. Remove the foil from the bowl of mixed fruit. Arrange the fruit over the cheese and garnish with strips of orange.

Serves 4–6

Champagne Summer Berries

Preparation time: 15 minutes
Cooking time: 3–5 minutes, plus chilling

- 250 g/8 oz strawberries,
  hulled and halved
- 250 g/8 oz raspberries
- 125 g/4 oz redcurrants,
  topped and tailed
- 125 g/4 oz blueberries,
  topped and tailed

- 25 g/1 oz caster sugar
- 4 tablespoons lemon juice
- 250 ml/8 fl oz chilled
  Champagne
- mint sprigs, to decorate
- almond biscuits, to serve

1 Mix the berries together in a pudding bowl. Sprinkle them with half of the sugar and half of the lemon juice. Set aside for *10 minutes.*

2 Meanwhile pour the remaining sugar on to a large plate. Dip the rims of four glass dessert bowls into the remaining lemon juice, shake off the excess, then dip each dish into the sugar. The sugar will cling to the lemon juice, making an attractive frosted rim.

3 Cover the pudding basin with kitchen foil and tie down. Place in a steamer or covered pan half-filled with boiling water and steam for *3–5 minutes.*

4 To serve, spoon the fruit into the prepared dishes being careful not to spoil the frosted rim. At the table, pour the chilled champagne on to the fruit and decorate with mint sprigs. Serve with almond biscuits.

Serves 4

Special Photography:
David Munns
Jacket Photography:
Sean Myers
Other Photography:
Reed Consumer Books Ltd./
William Adams-Lingwood /
Steve Baxter/Nick Carman/
Laurie Evans/Gus Filgate/
Christopher Hill/Graham Kirk/
Sandra Lane /David Loftus/
Diana Miller/Hilary Moore/
James Murphy/Peter Myers /
Sean Myers/Clive Streeter/
Philip Webb
Special Photography Home
Economist:
Oona van den Berg